John Indermaur, Charles Thwaites

The Student's Guide to Procedure

In the Queen's Bench Division of the High Court and to the Law of

Evidence

John Indermaur, Charles Thwaites

The Student's Guide to Procedure
In the Queen's Bench Division of the High Court and to the Law of Evidence

ISBN/EAN: 9783337168827

Printed in Europe, USA, Canada, Australia, Japan

Cover: Foto ©Suzi / pixelio.de

More available books at **www.hansebooks.com**

THE

STUDENT'S GUIDE

PROCEDURE

IN THE QUEEN'S BENCH DIVISION OF THE HIGH COURT

AND TO THE LAW OF

EVIDENCE.

BY

JOHN INDERMAUR, Solicitor,

(First Prizeman, Michaelmas, 1872),

AUTHOR OF " PRINCIPLES OF COMMON LAW," " MANUAL OF EQUITY," " MANUAL OF PRACTICE.
JOINT AUTHOR WITH MR. THWAITES OF
" THE STUDENT'S GUIDE TO REAL AND PERSONAL PROPERTY," &c., &c.

AND

CHARLES THWAITES, Solicitor,

*(First in First Class Honours, June, 1880; Sheffield District Prizeman, 1880;
Reardon (Yearly) Prizeman, 1880; Scott Scholar, 1880, and
Conveyancing Gold Medallist, 1880),*

AUTHOR OF " A GUIDE TO CRIMINAL LAW,"
JOINT AUTHOR WITH MR. INDERMAUR OF
" THE STUDENT'S GUIDE TO REAL AND PERSONAL PROPERTY," &c., &c.

LONDON:
GEO. BARBER, "LAW STUDENTS' JOURNAL" OFFICE,
16 & 17, CURSITOR STREET, CHANCERY LANE.

1894.

ADVERTISEMENT.

———◆———

THIS little work forms one of a series of Guides to the Bar Final by the Authors. The others are—on Real and Personal Property, third edition, by Messrs. Indermaur and Thwaites; on Criminal Law, third edition, by Mr. Thwaites; on Common Law, third edition, by Mr. Indermaur; on Trusts and Partnerships, second edition, by Mr. Indermaur; and on Specific Performances and Mortgages by Messrs. Indermaur and Thwaites. The two Guides last named are now obsolete, but Messrs. Indermaur and Thwaites have in preparation a new Guide on the Principles of Equity generally.

It is hoped that this Guide will be found of use by the class for whom it is written. Though particularly intended for Bar Students, it may, perhaps, be found of service to Articled Clerks as well.

Messrs. Indermaur and Thwaites continue to prepare Students in class, privately, and by post, for the Bar Final Examinations, Solicitors' Final (Pass and Honours) Examinations, and Solicitors' Intermediate Examination. Particulars may be had on application, personally or by letter, to Messrs. Indermaur and Thwaites, at their Chambers, 22, Chancery Lane, London, W.C.

22, CHANCERY LANE, LONDON,
May, 1894.

CONTENTS.

THE STUDENT'S GUIDE

TO

PROCEDURE

IN THE QUEEN'S BENCH DIVISION OF THE
HIGH COURT OF JUSTICE,

AND TO THE LAW OF

EVIDENCE GENERALLY.

INTRODUCTORY AND GENERAL.

FOR some time past the regulations at the Bar Final have permitted students to select four papers out of a total of six as their subjects for this examination, and one of the subjects that can be selected is Procedure and Evidence. This is the present state of things, but at and subsequently to Easter, 1895, when the new arrangements (issued on 5th March, 1894) come into force, all students must take up the subject of Procedure and Evidence. It appears to us, therefore, that the time has arrived when a Guide on these subjects will be of very general utility to Bar students. This small work is, therefore, specially framed with a view to the Bar Final, but at the same time it may be of service to students for the Solicitors' Final.

The bare heading " Procedure and Evidence " is somewhat vague, leaving it doubtful whether it includes all matters of Procedure and all matters of Evidence, or only Civil Procedure and Evidence, or at any rate only Procedure in the Queen's Bench Division. We are, however, assisted in coming to a conclusion by the announcement that is made, that students will only be examined in all matters so far as they have been treated in the lectures and classes during the two years preceding each examination. Now, the lectures have dealt with Procedure in the Queen's Bench Division, and with Criminal Procedure and Principles, but not with Procedure in the Chancery Division. Evidence has been dealt with generally. We have come to the conclusion in this work to deal not only with Procedure in the Queen's Bench Division, but with Evidence generally. We omit all special reference to Chancery Procedure, because that never has been lectured on yet. We omit all special reference to Criminal Procedure and Principles, because there is another book of the same style as this present one, which deals generally with Criminal Law and Procedure (*), and students can get all they require from that. Besides, we may observe that, to some extent, the Principles of Criminal Law have been lectured on, and such simple questions as the difference between Larceny and False Pretences have been asked; and we should not be surprised at any time to see an announcement of a Criminal paper being set. To a limited extent students should, therefore, get up Principles of Criminal Law as well as Criminal Procedure, and, therefore, we have decided in this work not to deal with Criminal Procedure, but to leave students to get that up from Thwaites' Guide to Criminal Law. As regards Evidence, there is so little distinctively applicable to Criminal matters as opposed to Civil matters, that we have come to the conclusion to deal with that subject generally.

Now, firstly, then, taking the subject of Procedure in the Queen's Bench Division of the High Court, we recommend students to read this first from Indermaur's Manual of

---

* A Guide to Criminal Law. By Charles Thwaites. Published by G. Barber, 16, Cursitor Street, E.C. 3rd edition, 1891. Price 5s.

Practice (*). This work contains Queen's Bench and Chancery Practice, and the part relating to the latter may be omitted. The student should read Parts I. & II., viz., pp. 1-181. Then it would also be advisable to read Part IV. on Appeals, being pp. 269-283. We think that a very thorough knowledge of Procedure will be gained from this book, but, of course, it will be of assistance to have the Annual Practice by one's side for occasional reference. It is not always easy for those who have seen no practice to grasp statements in text books, and a reference to the Rules of Court is sometimes of great assistance.

As an introduction to the Practice we have given in this work a slight elementary sketch of Queen's Bench Practice. We have also given a set of Test Questions on the portions of Indermaur's Manual of Practice which we (at present) advise should be read. We recommend that this set of Test Questions should from time to time be used whilst reading the book. Finally, we have given a carefully prepared Digest of Questions and Answers, mainly selected from the Questions set during a number of years at the Bar Final. This Digest of Questions and Answers should form the student's final reading, and we feel convinced that if he will thoroughly follow out the course we have indicated, he will be able to satisfactorily cope with any examination on the subject, and will at the same time have attained a very sound knowledge on the subject.

Now, secondly, taking the subject of Evidence, we believe the lecturer recommends Taylor on Evidence (8th edition, 1885), Broom's Maxims, and Stephen's Digest. Taylor is a large work in two volumes; and Best's Principles of Evidence (8th edition, 1893), also covers some 620 pages. Powell's Law of Evidence (6th edition, 1892), is a useful book, but it contains 669 pages. The two handy books on

---

* 6th edition. Published by Stevens & Haynes, Bell Yard, London. Price 14s.

the Law of Evidence are (1) Phipson's Law of Evidence, published by Stevens & Haynes in 1892, 430 pages, price 10s. 6d., and (2) Stephen's Digest of the Law of Evidence, 5th edition, published in 1887 by Macmillan, in 209 pages, price 6s. We recommend the Bar student to read (1) the chapter on Evidence at the end of Indermaur's Principles of Common Law ; (2) either Stephen's Digest or Phipson's ; and (3) to conclude with a revision of the Questions and Answers on Evidence which we publish herein, and which include all the Questions hitherto set on this subject at the Bar Final. We also give a series of Test Questions on Stephen's Digest, as we know from a wide experience that is the work chiefly affected by students, and these Questions should be carefully worked through by all students when reading their text book.

We now proceed to give the several matters we have named, i.e. :—

PROCEDURE—

1. An Elementary Sketch of Common Law Practice.
2. Test Questions on Indermaur's Manual of Practice, Parts I., II., and IV.
3. Digest of Questions and Answers on Procedure.

EVIDENCE—

1. Test Questions on Stephen's Digest of Evidence.
2. Digest of Questions and Answers on Evidence.

PROCEDURE.

I.—AN ELEMENTARY SKETCH OF COMMON LAW PRACTICE.

Prior to the Judicature Acts there were in existence distinct Courts, viz. :—(1) The Courts of Common Law, and (2) The Court of Chancery. The Courts of Common Law were older in their origin than the Court of Chancery, being, indeed, the outcome of that very ancient body, the Aula Regis. They were three in number, viz., the Court of Queen's Bench, the Court of Common Pleas, and the Court of Exchequer. The Court of Chancery was of later date, and arose from the defects of the Common Law, for in many cases the strictness and rigour of the Common Law rendered it unable to give relief, and it became necessary to apply to the King in person for aid, and the monarch deputing the matter to the Chancellor, the practice gradually grew up of applying to the Chancellor direct, so that Equity may be said to have had its origin to supply the defects of the Common Law, and to give relief where the Common Law was incompetent to do so, at least without circuity of action or multiplicity of suits.

The Judicature Acts, 1873 and 1875, had for their object the fusing of the Courts of Common Law and Equity into one, and causing the same rules to be observed in each, it being specially provided that where there was found to be a difference between the rules of Law and of Equity, the rules of Equity should prevail. The Judicature Acts came into operation on the 1st of November, 1875.

The " Supreme Court of Judicature " is constituted by the union of the various former Courts, viz. : (1) The Court of Chancery; (2) the Court of Queen's Bench; (3) the Court of Common Pleas; (4) the Court of Exchequer; (5) the Court of Admiralty; (6) the Court of Probate; and (7) the Divorce Court; and this Supreme Court is separated into two permanent sections, viz.: "The High Court of Justice" and "Her Majesty's Court of Appeal." The High Court of Justice is separated into Divisions as follows: (1) the Chancery Division; (2) the Queen's Bench Division; and (3) the Probate, Divorce and Admiralty Division, being indeed, divisions analogous in the main to the previous Courts. Certain matters are within the exclusive jurisdiction of a particular division, but if the action is brought in the wrong division it can be transferred, or retained there. To facilitate the prosecution in country districts of certain proceedings in an action, provision has been made for the establishment throughout the country of District Registries, where actions may be commenced and continued down to entry for trial.

Proceedings in the High Court of Justice are commenced by an action, the first step in which is a writ of summons. This writ of summons commands the defendant to appear within eight days, and indorsed on it are particulars of the plaintiff's claim. In certain cases the plaintiff may specially indorse his writ under Order III., rule 6, viz., where the action is for a liquidated sum under some contract or statute or trust, or for the recovery of land by a landlord against his tenant holding over after the expiration of his tenancy.

The advantages a plaintiff derives from specially indorsing a writ are two, viz. :—(1) The special indorsement operates as a statement of claim, and no further statement of claim can be required or is, in fact, allowed to be delivered; (2) Even if the defendant does appear, on an affidavit of good cause of action, and that defendant has only appeared for the purpose of delay, unless good cause is shown, an order may be made for the plaintiff to have judgment notwithstanding the appearance. An application for such an order is called a summons under Order XIV. On the hearing of such a summons, if the Master or Judge gives leave to defend, he may, if he thinks no prolonged hearing is necessary, direct the action to at once be set down for trial in a special list. The writ is served personally on a defendant if possible, but if personal service cannot be effected an order may be obtained for substituted service. The writ only remains in force for twelve months, but it may be renewed from time to time on showing that reasonable efforts have been made to serve it, or for other good reasons. The defendant, personally, or by his solicitor, should enter an appearance and serve on plaintiff's solicitor a duplicate of the sealed memorandum of appearance, together with a notice of appearance, within eight days. If an infant is a party to an action, he sues by next friend, and defends by guardian *ad litem*. If the defendant does not appear judgment may be entered against him, which will be a final judgment if the claim is for a liquidated amount, and if for an unliquidated amount then interlocutory judgment, after which a Writ of Inquiry must be issued to assess the amount of the damages.

Taking it that the defendant appears, and no application is made under Order XIV. or that such an application is unsuccessful, and the case has not been directed to be put in the special list for speedy trial, we next have the pleadings, the object of which is to show to the Court and jury the questions in issue between the parties, and the facts on which they respectively rely. These pleadings are as follows :—

Statement of claim by plaintiff, to be delivered within six weeks from appearance, or if the defendant demands a statement of claim, which he may do on appearance or within eight days therefrom, then within five weeks of such demand. It contains a plain statement of the plaintiff's case and what he asks.

Statement of defence by defendant within ten days of the delivery of the statement of claim. It contains a plain statement of defendant's case. It may also contain a counter-claim against the plaintiff.

Statement of reply by defendant within three weeks of the defence, which, usually, simply contains joinder of issue, that is, a traverse or denial of what is stated by the defendant. If, however, the statement of defence contained a counter-claim, then substantially the reply is, as to that, the plaintiff's defence, and then for the purpose of joining issue another pleading is required, and it is—

The rejoinder by defendant within four days of the reply.

No pleading after reply except joinder of issue is allowed without special leave.

It must, however, be noticed that it is now provided that a plaintiff may indorse on his writ a statement sufficient to give notice of his claim, and may state that if the defendant appears he intends to proceed to trial without pleadings. In such a case, unless an order is made on the application of the defendant, for pleadings to be delivered notwithstanding this notice, the plaintiff may within ten days of appearance give a twenty-one days notice of trial without pleadings, and the action is at once set down for trial.

Assuming, however, that there are pleadings, as soon as issue is joined the pleadings are then said to be closed, and the next step is for the plaintiff to give notice of trial, which he must do within six weeks from the close of the pleadings. The notice is a ten days' one, unless the defendant is under terms to take " short notice," and it is then four days. The cause must then be entered for trial.

With regard to the pleadings, certain points are to be specially observed. They are to be as brief as possible, divided into paragraphs, numbered consecutively, each paragraph relating, as far as may be, to a distinct subject matter; a mere general denial is not sufficient, but every matter specifically alleged by a party, must be specifically met, otherwise it will be deemed to be admitted. With regard, however, to an action for recovery of land, if the defendant's defence is of a legal nature, it is always sufficient for him simply to plead that he is in possession, without dealing with every particular allegation made by the plaintiff in his statement of claim. The signature of counsel to a pleading is not necessary, but where pleadings have been settled by counsel, they are to be signed by him, and if not so settled, they are to be signed by the solicitor for the party, or by the party himself if he sues or defends in person. The plaintiff, in his statement of claim, may state where the action is to be tried, and if he states no place, it is tried in Middlesex, but this is subject to the defendant's right to take out a summons to change the place of the trial, and he may obtain an order if he can show that he cannot obtain a fair trial in the particular place by reason of local prejudice, or that it is more convenient and a saving of expense to have it elsewhere.

If the defendant fails to put in a defence, judgment may be signed against him in just the same way as if he had not appeared.

Taking it, however, that a defence is put in, and issue joined, the next thing is, as already mentioned, to proceed to the trial of the action, and notice of trial is given as already mentioned. In cases of slander, libel, false imprisonment, malicious prosecution, seduction, and breach of promise of marriage, the plaintiff may give notice of trial before a judge and jury, and if he gives notice of trial before a judge alone, the defendant may, within four days, give notice requiring a jury; but in all other cases if a jury is desired, a summons to have the case tried by a jury must be taken out within ten days of service of notice of trial. Notice of trial having been given, and the cause duly entered for trial, the parties then prepare for trial by issuing and serving all necessary subpœnas, preparing their briefs, &c., and ultimately the cause comes on to be heard, when verdict is given, followed by the judgment of the Court.

The judgment may be enforced in various different ways, *e.g.*, by *fieri facias*, for the purpose of seizing and selling the debtor's goods, *elegit* for the purpose of seizing his lands, or by a *garnishee* order, which is an order obtained against some third person who owes money to the judgment debtor, commanding him to pay the same to the judgment creditor instead, so as to satisfy his claim.

Thus then the action is brought to a close, but there are a few special matters to mention.

Sometimes, instead of delivering the ordinary pleading as to facts, the plaintiff or defendant desires to dispute the sufficiency in law of the pleading of his opponent. Formerly in such a case he would have delivered a demurrer, but now he puts in his pleading in the ordinary manner, raising therein the point of law, which may either be determined at the trial, or be ordered to be disposed of before or after the trial.

Interrogatories are a set of questions delivered by one party to the other, and which are required to be answered on oath within ten days. In all cases an order must be obtained for their delivery. Discovery of documents may also be obtained by either party to an action by applying by summons without filing any affidavit in support thereof, asking for an order for his opponent to make an affidavit as to what documents are or have been in his possession, custody, or power, relating to the matters in question in the action. Before delivery of any interrogatories, or before the hearing of any summons for discovery of documents, it is necessary to pay into Court, as security for costs, the sum of £5, and with regard to interrogatories, if their length exceeds 5 folios, the further sum of 10s. for every additional folio.

Numerous other interlocutory steps may be necessary to be taken in any particular action according to circumstances, *e.g.*, summons for time to deliver any pleading, summons for further particulars of the plaintiff's claim or the defendant's counter-claim, amendment of pleadings, payment of money into Court, &c., &c.

II.—TEST QUESTIONS ON PARTS I., II., AND IV., OF INDERMAUR'S MANUAL OF PRACTICE. 6TH EDITION.

(The figures at the end of each question signify the pages where the answers may be found.)

PART I.

1. Give a short explanation of the origin of the former Courts of Common Law and Chancery, together with some account of the proceedings in such Courts. (1-8.)

2. How is the High Court of Justice now constituted under the Judicature Acts, and what jurisdiction is vested therein? (10-12.)

3. State some of the matters which now, under the Judicature Acts, are specially assigned to the Chancery Division. (13, 14.)

4. State shortly how the Court of Appeal is now constituted, and what jurisdiction is vested therein. (18, 19.)

5. Enumerate some of the matters in which the Masters have no jurisdiction. (21, note *s*.)

6. What are the functions of the chief clerks of the Chancery Division? Mention any matters in which they have no jurisdiction. (23, 24.)

7. How did the House of Lords acquire its jurisdiction as a Court of Appeal, and how is it now constituted as such a Court under the Appellate Jurisdiction Act 1876? (27, 28.)

8. What is the consequence at the present day of non-joinder or mis-joinder of plaintiffs or defendants in an action?   (30, 31.)

9. When property is vested in trustees, executors, or administrators, and an action is brought concerning the same, is it necessary to make the beneficiaries parties, or are they sufficiently represented by such trustees, &c.?   (32.)

10. Explain shortly the practice of consolidation of actions, and give two instances in which such consolidation may take place.   (32, 33.)

11. A sues B. B has a claim against A and X on a joint contract. Can he counter-claim in the action in respect of this claim?   (33-35.)

12. What do you understand by third party procedure? Detail shortly the practice.   (34, 35.)

13. If, in the course of an action, the plaintiff or defendant dies, but the cause of action still continues, what course should be taken by the surviving party? If the deceased has no personal representative, can the action possibly be proceeded with?   (36, 37.)

14. Generally speaking, different causes of action can be united in the same writ. What are the exceptions to this rule?   (38.)

15. How do the following persons respectively sue and defend:—Infants, married women, persons of unsound mind, and corporations?   (39, 40.)

16. How are actions comprising matters of a public nature commenced?   (40.)

17. State shortly the practice as to suing *in formâ pauperis*. Where the plaintiff sues *in formâ pauperis* and succeeds, what costs is he entitled to?   (40, 41.)

18. In an action brought against a justice of the peace or a constable in respect of anything done by him in the exercise of his office, does any, and if so what, preliminary have to be observed before commencing the action?   (41.)

PART II.

19. What indorsements does an ordinary writ of summons contain? Under what circumstances may a writ be specially indorsed, and what is the great advantage of a special indorsement? (42-45.)

20. How are writs served on the following parties respectively:—Infants, lunatics, registered companies, and partners? (46-49.)

21. In an action of ejectment the defendant cannot be found, and the premises are vacant. Under these circumstances how may the writ be served? (49.)

22. Under what circumstances may a writ be issued against a defendant who is abroad out of the jurisdiction of the Court? (50-52, and see supplemental note.)

23. What is meant by a concurrent writ? Give an instance of an action in which a concurrent writ would properly be issued. (53.)

24. Within what time must a defendant appear to a writ of summons? What is the effect of a defendant appearing, but omitting to give notice of appearance? (53-55.)

25. A makes a lease of premises to B. X, who contends that the property belongs to him and not to A, brings an action of ejectment against B. What is B's duty, and what course may A take? (56.)

26. What is the consequence of a defendant not appearing to a writ of summons? Distinguish in your answer between a writ for a fixed liquidated amount, and a writ to recover unliquidated damages. (59-62.)

27. A sues B, an infant, and duly serves the writ. B does not appear. Can A sign judgment, and if not, what course should he take? (63.)

28. What is the object of a summons under Order XIV.? With regard to a summons under Order XIV., what course may a Master now take, if he gives unconditional liberty

to defend, with a view to the speedy trial of the action?
(63-67.)

29.   Plaintiff sues in the High Court to recover £40, and
gets judgment for this amount on a summons under Order
XIV.   What costs is he entitled to?   (65.)

30.   If a defendant desires in the course of an action
to consent to judgment, how is such consent given (*a*) if
he has appeared by a solicitor, (*b*) if he has appeared in
person?   (67.)

31.   What is the object of pleadings in an action?   Can
an action ever proceed to trial without pleadings?   If so,
detail the course of procedure.   (68, 69.)

32.   A defendant is sued for a debt.   Is it sufficient for
him to plead " never indebted "?   (70, 71, 76.)

33.   Within what time must a Statement of Claim be
delivered in an action?   If not so delivered, what course may
a defendant take?   (73-75.)

34.   How is it determined at what place an action is to
be tried?   Has the defendant any voice in the matter, or is
the place of trial entirely in the choice of the plaintiff?   (75,
111.)

35.   In an action brought to recover a debt, is it open to
the defendant to set off or counter-claim for unliquidated
damages in (*a*) contract (*b*) tort?   (78.)

36.   Within what time must a Statement of Defence be
put in?   What is the consequence of the defendant omitting
to put in a Statement of Defence?   Distinguish in your
answer between actions for fixed liquidated amounts, and for
unliquidated damages respectively.   (79, 80.)

37.   What do you understand by " joinder of issue," and
in what pleading is joinder of issue usually contained?   (81.)

38.   Within what time must a Statement of Reply be put
in, and what is the consequence of a Reply not being put in?
Hereon, what difference would you notice if the defendant's
defence contained a counter-claim?   (81, 82.)

39. What was a demurrer? What course is now taken instead of demurring? (82, 83.)

40. Can a defence which did not exist when the writ was issued, but which has only arisen since the action was brought, be set up? (84, 85.)

41. Under what circumstances may a pleading be amended without leave? When an amendment is made without leave, what is the position of the other party with regard to his pleading? (85-87.)

42. At what stage of an action may a notice be given to admit facts, and within what time should admissions be made? What is the consequence of refusing or neglecting to admit facts under such a notice? (87.)

43. In an action of ejectment the defendant simply pleads that he is in possession; what matters is he entitled to go into at the trial under such a defence? (88.)

44. How are interlocutory applications in the course of an action made? Can a notice of motion be served upon a defendant before he has appeared to the writ? (89, 90.)

45. On the hearing of a summons in chambers, is either party entitled to attend by counsel, and if so, what is the position with regard to the extra costs thus occasioned? (91.)

46. What do you understand by a summons for directions, and what are its advantages? Can such a summons be taken out in the Chancery Division? (92, 93.)

47. Enumerate any orders which need not be formally drawn up. (93, 94.)

48. In what actions, and at what stage, may a defendant pay money into Court? If he has so paid money into Court, when is the plaintiff entitled to take it out? Distinguish in your answer between cases in which the defendant admits his liability, and cases in which he denies his liability. (95-99.)

49. On the trial of an action in which money has been

paid into Court, ought the jury to be informed that such a payment has been made or not? (99.)

50. When may interrogatories be administered in an action; and within what time, and how, must they be answered? (100-102.)

51. How do you obtain discovery of documents in an action? Sketch the outline of an ordinary affidavit of documents. (102, 296.)

52. How do you obtain inspection of documents? If certain of the documents consist of business books, is the party always obliged to produce the original books for inspection, or what course may he take instead? (104-106.)

53. How is an order for discovery served, and what are the consequences of disobedience to such an order? (107.)

54. With regard to discovery generally, what provision has been made for securing the costs of the party against whom discovery is obtained? (107-109.)

55. Under what circumstances may an action of contract brought in the High Court be transferred to the County Court, and at what stage of the action should an application for such transfer be made? (110, 111.)

56. Mention three cases in which the defendant may properly apply to dismiss the action for want of prosecution. (112.)

57. Can the plaintiff under any and what circumstances obtain an order for the arrest of the defendant during the action? (112, 113.)

58. Under what circumstances may an action, brought in the District Registry, be removed to London, and state how the removal is effected? Can an action ever be removed from London to a District Registry? (114, 115.)

59. Mention the chief cases in which the plaintiff may be ordered to give security for the costs of an action. Is it any ground for obtaining security that the plaintiff is residing in Scotland or Ireland? (115-118.)

60. Explain what is meant by process of interpleader. What is the nature of the affidavit which must be filed in support of an interpleader summons? (118, 119.)

61. Detail shortly the procedure on an interpleader summons. Is there any appeal in interpleader matters? (120, 121.)

62. What is a special case, and under what circumstances may this mode of procedure be properly resorted to? (121, 122.)

63. Explain the following expressions:—" Costs, costs in the cause," and "plaintiff's costs in any event." (123.)

64. How and within what time may appeals be brought respectively from a decision of a Master, a District Registrar, and a Judge sitting in chambers? (123, 124.)

65. A obtains an order for judgment against B on a summons under Order XIV., but neglects to sign judgment, and lets more than a year go by without doing so, but now wishes to sign judgment. How must he proceed? (124.)

66. What do you understand by a notice of discontinuance? When a notice of discontinuance has been given, can another action be brought in respect of the same subject matter? (124, 125.)

67. An action is brought for a penalty under a statute. The defendant proposes terms, and the plaintiff desires to compromise. Can he do so? (126.)

68. When should notice of trial be given in an action? What is the length of such notice, and what is the position with regard to a jury? (128, 129.)

69. Within what time must a cause be entered for trial? Can a notice of trial once given be counter-manded? (130.)

70. What is the object of giving (a) a notice to produce, (b) a notice to inspect and admit, before going to trial? (131, 132.)

71. What are the rules with regard to the employment

of more than one counsel at the trial of an action, and with regard to the payment of refreshers to counsel? (133, 134.)

72. What is the difference between a *subpœna ad testificandum* and a *subpœna duces tecum?* How do you secure the attendance (*a*) of a witness residing in Scotland, (*b*) of a witness residing in France, (*c*) of a witness who is in custody? (135, 136.)

73. What do you understand by a summons to take evidence *de bene esse?* (136, 137.)

74. Give a short outline of the procedure at the trial of an action. Who has the right to begin at the trial? (138, 139.)

75. What is the difference between a general and a special verdict? (140.)

76. A trial is postponed on the terms that the applicant pays the " costs of the day." Explain what is meant by this expression. (140.)

77. What is meant (*a*) by withdrawing a juror, (*b*) by the plaintiff being non-suited? Explain the position as to costs in both cases. (140, 141.)

78. The plaintiff in an action is an infant suing by his next friend, and a verdict is recovered. To whom would the amount be paid by the defendant? (144.)

79. Mention some of the chief grounds for moving for a new trial. To what tribunal is the motion made, and within what time? (145-147.)

80. Under what circumstances is a plaintiff able to issue execution upon a judgment without leave? Is there any limit as to the time within which leave can be granted? How long does a writ of execution remain in force? (148, 149.)

81. Mention the different ways in which judgments may be enforced. Explain the difference between a writ of *elegit* and equitable execution. (149-161.)

82. State shortly the practice to get equitable execution,

and give the nature of the affidavit to be filed in support of the application. (154.)

83. What is a garnishee order and how is it obtained? What is the nature of the affidavit which has to be filed in support of the application for such an order? (156.)

84. A has a judgment against B, and he ascertains that B is entitled to certain bank stock and railway shares. How would he avail himself of this property towards satisfaction of his judgment? (158.)

85. A has judgment against X, who is a member of the firm of Brown & Co. How can A avail himself of X's interest in this firm towards the satisfaction of his judgment? (158.)

86. In what different ways may a judgment for the recovery of property other than land or money be enforced? (159.)

87. An order or judgment directs a defendant to do a certain thing, or to pay money, by a certain date. How ought the order to be served, and what memorandum should be endorsed thereon? (159, 160.)

88. What do you understand by a judgment *quando acciderint*, and how is such a judgment enforced? (163, 164.)

89. Under what circumstances may judgments of inferior Courts be removed to the High Court for the purposes of execution? (164.)

90. State the general rule as to costs in an action in the High Court; distinguish between cases tried by a Judge alone, and cases tried by a Judge and jury. (165, 166.)

91. Summarise the chief provisions of the County Courts Act 1888, on the subject of costs in High Court actions. (166, 167.)

92. A recovers in an action of debt in the High Court £25; B recovers in an action for assault in the High Court £5; C recovers in an action for libel in the High Court 40s. Each action is tried before a judge and jury, and no special

directions as to costs are given. What is the position, as regards costs, in each case? (167, 168.)

93. A plaintiff sues in the High Court for £35 owing on contract. The defendant defends, and also counter-claims for £100. The plaintiff recovers the amount he sued for, and also succeeds on the counter-claim. To what costs is he entitled? (168.)

94. Has the Court any jurisdiction, (a) to order an entirely successful plaintiff to pay the defendant's costs, (b) to order an entirely successful defendant to pay the plaintiff's costs? (169.)

95. What notice of appointment to tax costs is required to be given? Under what circumstances may costs be taxed on the higher scale? What is meant by an "affidavit of increase"? (170.)

96. Explain and illustrate the difference between "solicitor and client" costs, and "party and party" costs? (171.)

97. Within what time must a client obtain an order to tax his own solicitor's bill? What is the rule with regard to the costs of the taxation? (172, 173.)

98. State shortly the procedure to review a taxation of costs. (174.)

99. What is meant by arbitration? What statute governs the subject of arbitration generally? (176.)

100. Explain the two different ways in which, under the Arbitration Act 1889, matters may be referred by the Court. What is the rule with regard to the costs of referred matters? (177, 178.)

101. Where there has been a compulsory reference, what appeal lies from the award, and to what tribunal? (178.)

102. A and B are partners, and the partnership deed contains the usual arbitration clause. Disputes having arisen between them, A commences an action. Can B in

any, and if so, what way compel A to have the matter disposed of by arbitration ? (178, 179.)

103. Define "submission to arbitration." To how many arbitrators may a matter be submitted ? Within what times must the arbitrators and their umpire respectively make their award ? (179.)

104. How may the attendance of a witness be compelled before an arbitrator? (180.)

105. If arbitrators who should appoint an umpire neglect to do so, how may an umpire be appointed ? (180.)

106. How may points of law arising in the course of an arbitration be determined by the Court ? (181.)

107. How may an arbitrator's award be enforced ? (181.)

PART IV.

108. Within what time must an appeal now be brought to Her Majesty's Court of Appeal? What length of notice of appeal must be given ? (269-270.)

109. Under what circumstances will an appellant be ordered to give security for the costs of an appeal ? (271.)

110. The plaintiff in an action appeals and the defendant also desires at the hearing to contend that the decision should on a certain point be varied. Is it necessary for him to bring a cross appeal, or what course must he take ? (272.)

111. How is the evidence in the Court below brought before the Court of Appeal on the hearing of an appeal ? Can the Court receive new evidence? (272-273.)

112. What powers has the Court of Appeal as regards : (a) amendment ; (b) inferences of fact ; (c) costs? (273.)

113. Before how many judges is an appeal heard? What is the extent of the powers of one judge of the Court of Appeal sitting alone ? (274, 275.)

114. Does an appeal act as a stay of execution? If an appeal, in fact, delays execution, is interest allowed on the amount which should have been paid ? (275.)

115. To whom and in what manner is an appeal brought from a decision of a judge sitting in chambers in the Chancery Division? (275.)

116. Enumerate some orders which are not subject to appeal. (276.)

117. Can an action ever be maintained in the nature of a Bill of Review? (276, 277.)

118. Give a short sketch of the proceedings by way of appeal to the House of Lords. (278-280.)

119. To what tribunal are appeals made from an inferior Court, as for instance a County Court, and within what time must such appeals be brought? What notice of appeal has to be given? (281-282.)

120. Does an appeal from a County Court operate as a stay of execution? Can the parties bind themselves by agreement not to appeal? (282.)

III.—DIGEST OF QUESTIONS AND ANSWERS.

1.—PRELIMINARY.

Q. Mention the principal matters for consideration before commencing an action, giving an illustration in each case.

A. I should consider firstly whether there was a cause of action, in other words whether there was an *injuria*, the rule being *damnum absque injuriâ* will not sustain an action. Then I should consider, even if there were a right of action, whether it was of a substantial kind and worth suing for, for although the rule is that *injuria sine damno* will sustain an action, yet it is not usually worth while to bring an action unless both *injuria* and *damnum* are combined, for there is the risk of not recovering sufficient to entitle the plaintiff to his costs. An instance of the rule that *damnum absque injuriâ* will not sustain an action is found in the case of Chasemore v. Richards (7 H. L. C., 349); and an instance of the rule that *injuria sine damno* will sustain an action is found in the case of Ashby v. White (Indermaur's Common Law Cases, 27). See also hereon Indermaur's Principles of Common Law, 3-5. Another important matter for consideration before commencing the action is the parties to sue and to be sued. (See Indermaur's Practice, 30, 31.)

Q. What is the effect of mis-joinder or non-joinder of parties?

A. Neither is now in any way fatal to the action. As to non-joinder, parties may be joined by leave of the Court, but if as plaintiffs their consent must be given. As to mis-joinder, judgment may be given for or against such one or more as may be found entitled or found liable without any amendment, or the Court may order the names of any parties improperly joined to be struck out. A defendant is, however, entitled to any extra costs occasioned by the plaintiff's mis-joinder. (Indermaur's Practice, 30, 31.)

Q. State the leading rule as to joining in one action claims in respect of several causes of action—with reference both to the nature of the claim and to the capacities of the parties.

A. The general rule is that different causes of action may be joined in one action, but if it appears to the Court or a judge that they cannot be conveniently tried together separate trials may be ordered. Except, however, by special leave, an action for recovery of land cannot be joined with any other cause of action, except mesne profits, arrears of rent, or double value in respect of the premises, or damages for the breach of any contract under which the premises are held. Claims by a trustee in bankruptcy cannot be joined with claims in any other capacity except by special leave, and claims by or against executors or administrators, as such, may only be joined with personal claims when they arise out of the estate. (Indermaur's Practice, 38.)

Q. *Are there any, and if any, what limits to the jurisdiction of the High Court of Justice to entertain actions or suits?*

A. The jurisdiction only extends to England and Wales and the town of Berwick-on-Tweed; but even as regards causes of action arising abroad, the Court may, acting *in personam*, take cognizance of them if the parties are here. (See Mostyn v. Fabrigas, Indermaur's Common Law Cases, 54; Penn v. Baltimore, Indermaur's Conveyancing and Equity Cases, 141.) In some cases also the Court may give leave to sue here though the defendant is abroad, under Order XI., rule 1. The Court has, however, no jurisdiction in an action for trespass to lands situate abroad (British South Africa Co. v. Compania di Moçambique, 63 L. J., Q. B., 70; 69 L. T., 604.) No action under the Employers Liability Act, or upon a County Court judgment, can be commenced in the High Court. The Court has no jurisdiction in actions against independent foreign rulers (Mighell v. Sultan of Johore, *Law Students' Journal*, January, 1894, p. 6).

Q. *In what cases is service out of the jurisdiction of a writ of summons allowed by a judge?*

A. Under Order XI., when the action is in respect of land within the jurisdiction, or defendant ordinarily resides within the jurisdiction, or the action is to administer the estate of a person who died domiciled in the jurisdiction, or is for an injunction as to anything within the jurisdiction, or the action is for breach within the jurisdiction of any contract (wherever made) which ought to be performed within the jurisdiction and the defendant is not domiciled or ordinarily resident in Scotland or Ireland. If the defendant is not a British subject, and is in a foreign territory, he is served with notice of the writ; if a British subject, with the writ. Leave to issue a writ against a defendant out of the jurisdiction can only be given by a Judge in person. (Indermaur's Practice, 50, 51.)

Q. What were the principal changes in procedure intro-duced by the Judicature Acts and Rules?

A. The idea was to fuse the former systems of law and equity. We find the old declaration, plea, and replication formerly existing at law, and the old bill of complaint and other steps formerly existing in the Court of Chancery abolished, and in substitution therefor we find a uniform procedure of statement of claim, statement of defence, and statement of reply. The pleadings are now divided into paragraphs numbered consecutively, and each paragraph, so far as can be, must deal with distinct matters, and pleadings must be printed if they exceed ten folios. Provisions have specially been made aiming at the brevity of pleadings. General allegations are not sufficient, but each matter alleged by the opponent must be met specifically, or will be taken to be omitted. Many other matters might be noticed, but the foregoing points may be fairly mentioned as the chief changes.

2.—Commencement of Action, Appearance, Judgment on Default of Appearance and under Order XIV.

Q. What is a writ of summons, and what are the different kinds of writ of summons, and what are the different modes of service?

A. A writ of summons is the mode by which an action in the High Court is commenced; it is dated on the day of its issue and indorsed with the nature of the claim made or relief required. It specifies the Division to which it is assigned, is addressed to the defendant, and commands him to appear within eight days after service. The different kinds of writ of summons are a writ with general indorsement, a specially indorsed writ, a writ for service out of the jurisdiction, and concurrent writs. The usual mode of service is by delivering a copy to defendant and producing the original, or by his solicitor indorsing on the writ acceptance of service and undertaking to appear. In cases of vacant possession, if personal service cannot be effected the writ is served by pasting a copy on the door or on a tree; and in any other case in which personal service cannot be effected, service may be made in the special way allowed by an order for substituted service. In the case of an infant defendant, the writ is served on the guardian or person with whom he resides. Where partners are sued in their partnership name, the writ is served on any partner or on the person in control at the principal place of business, in which case notice also must be served that the writ is delivered to him in that capacity.

Q. State shortly the procedure in an action from issue of writ until judgment.

A. Writ issued and served; appearance within eight days; statement of claim within six weeks of appearance, or within five weeks if demanded; statement of defence within ten days; statement of reply within 21 days. If a counterclaim there will be a rejoinder within four days of reply. Notice of trial within six weeks of the close of the pleadings. Entry for trial. Trial. Verdict and judgment. There may be various interlocutory steps according to circumstances, *e.g.*, summonses for time to take any steps, delivery of interrogatories, or obtaining discovery of documents. In some cases after defendant's appearance a speedy judgment may be obtained under the provisions of Order XIV. (See *post*, p. 31.)

Q. Describe the course of procedure in an action for recovery of land, pointing out the changes in the modern practice.

A. The procedure is generally the same as in ordinary

actions. The old form of action rested on a fiction in which the claimant was supposed to have demised the land to a tenant who had been ejected by the defendant. This fiction was swept away by the Common Law Procedure Act 1852, but the action of ejectment was still placed upon a footing peculiar to itself. Under the Judicature practice the term " ejectment " is still retained as the short title for an action for the recovery of land, but it is now generally governed by the ordinary rules applicable to all actions. It is, however, ordinarily sufficient in a statement of defence in such an action for the defendant to simply plead that he is in possession. (See *post*, pp. 33, 34.)

Q. How may infants and married women sue and be sued?

A. An infant sues by his next friend, and defends by his guardian *ad litem*. A married woman may now sue and be sued as provided by the Married Women's Property Act 1882—that is to say, as a *feme sole*. (Indermaur's Practice, 38, 39.)

Q. State the rules now in force for bringing and prosecuting an action against a firm consisting of several partners.

A. They may be sued in the firm's name without specifying the individuals ; and the writ may be served on any one of the partners, or on the person managing or having control at the principal place of business, but in this latter case a notice must also be served on such person stating that the writ is served on him in that capacity. The partners should then appear individually, but the proceedings continue in the firm's name. When judgment is obtained, execution may be issued against any of the direct partnership property, or against any person who has admitted that he is or has been adjudged a partner, or against any person who has been served as a partner and has failed to appear, and if the judgment creditor claims to be entitled to issue execution against any other person, as being a member of the firm, he may apply for leave to do so. (Indermaur's Practice, 47, 56, 162.)

Q. What course is open to the plaintiff when the defendant makes default in entering an appearance?

A. The plaintiff can sign judgment. If the action is for recovery of a fixed liquidated amount, or to recover land, the judgment will be final ; but if for unliquidated damages or detention of goods it will be interlocutory, and a writ of inquiry will then be issued to assess the damages. (Indermaur's Practice, 59, 61.)

Q. Have the rules under the Judicature Acts changed the previous practice as to proceeding with an action after death or bankruptcy of a party pending the action?

A. Yes, whereas, formerly, the action would have abated, now the action does not abate, but an order may, if necessary, be made *ex parte* for the personal representative, trustee, or other successor in interest (if any) to be made a party to the action, or to be served with notice thereof, and any such order may be made as may be just for the disposal of the action. The new party must enter an appearance as if served with a writ, but may apply within twelve days of service to discharge or vary any such order. (Indermaur's Practice, 36, 37.)

Q. Explain the terms " special indorsement," " demurrer," and " counter-claim."

A. Special indorsement consists of a statement of the plaintiff's claim with dates and items, constituting, in fact, the statement of claim in the action. The cases in which a writ may be specially indorsed are enumerated in Order III., rule 6, and the great advantage of a special indorsement is, that on the appearance of a defendant a summons for judgment under Order XIV. may be taken out. (Indermaur's Practice, 45.) A demurrer was the former mode of objecting to the sufficiency of an opponent's pleading in point of law. Now, no formal demurrer is allowed, but any such objection is taken in the party's pleading. (*Ib.*, 82.) Counter-claim signifies a claim set up in an action by a defendant against the plaintiff by means of which he may recover judgment against the plaintiff instead of bringing a cross action. (*Ib.*, 78.)

Q. Does a set-off under the Judicature Acts differ in any respect from a counter-claim ?

A. The terms are generally used as synonymous, but strictly set-off is a defence to the plaintiff's claim of such a nature that it might under the Statutes of Set-off have been set up prior to the Judicature practice, whilst a counter-claim may go beyond this, forming the subject of a claim which could formerly not have been set up, but for which a separate action must have been brought. A set-off strictly is only a defence, but a counter-claim goes beyond that, so that a defendant may recover judgment against the plaintiff. (Indermaur's Practice, 78.) There is also a distinction as to costs, for in cases coming within the County Courts Act 1888, if by reason of set-off the plaintiff only recovers a balance under the amounts named in that Act (see *post*, p. 52), the plaintiff will not get his costs without a certificate or order, whilst if the defendant's claim is a counter-claim as opposed to a set-off, the plaintiff will get his full costs, and the defendant any costs in respect of the counter-claim. (Indermaur's Practice, 168.)

Q. Explain the necessity for and meaning of " renewal of a writ of summons," and " concurrent writs." Is there at any stage of an action before judgment, any mode by which a defendant may be arrested ?

A. If a writ is not served within twelve months of its issue, the plaintiff, in order to prevent the operation of the Statutes of Limitation, or for other purposes, may, before the twelve months expire, renew the writ on proof that reasonable efforts have been made to effect service, or for other good reason, for six months, and so on from time to time ; it is renewed by being resealed (Indermaur's Practice,

52). *Concurrent writs* are simply duplicate originals issued to expedite service (*Ib.*, 53). Yes, under the Debtors Act 1869, where the plaintiff proves at any time before final judgment, on oath, to the satisfaction of a Judge, that he has a good cause of action for £50 at least, and there is reason to think the defendant is about to abscond, and (except in actions for penalties not arising out of contract) that his absence will materially prejudice the plaintiff in prosecuting his action, defendant may be imprisoned for not exceeding six months, unless and until he sooner gives the prescribed security. (Indermaur's Practice, 112, 113.)

Q. In what cases and by what process can a defendant obtain in an action relief against a third person not a party to the action ?

A. This question embraces the subject of third party procedure. A defendant can thus obtain relief where he claims contribution or indemnity upon a contract (express or implied), or upon equitable principles, against a person not a party to the action. The process is for the defendant within the time for delivering his defence, by leave of a Judge, to issue and serve a third party notice. The third party may appear to it within eight days, and if he does appear, directions are given as to mode of trial. If he does not appear, the defendant may let judgment go, and on satisfying it, enter judgment against the third party for the contribution or indemnity claimed by the notice. (Indermaur's Practice, 34-36.)

Q. In what cases may a writ of summons be specially indorsed, and what are the advantages of such indorsement ?

A. The writ may be specially indorsed, where the plaintiff is suing for a liquidated demand in money, arising (*a*) upon a contract expressed or implied; or (*b*) on a bond or contract under seal; or (*c*) on a statute; or (*d*) on a guarantee; or (*e*) on a trust; and also (*f*) in an action for recovery of land (with or without a claim for mesne profits) by a landlord against his tenant whose term has expired or been duly determined by notice to quit. The advantages of such indorsement are :—(1) That if the defendant appears, the plaintiff may apply for leave to sign judgment, notwithstanding the appearance, under Order XIV. ; and (2) no further statement of claim is required, or indeed allowed to be delivered, but the indorsement on the writ is to be deemed sufficient. (Indermaur's Practice, 44, 45.)

Q. Describe the procedure under Order XIV., explaining in what cases it is applicable.

A. An affidavit is made verifying the cause of action, and that defendant has no defence, and thereupon a summons is issued to show cause why judgment should not be signed, notwithstanding appearance. The summons must be served four clear days before the return day, and with it a copy of the affidavit, and of any exhibit thereto. If then the defendant does not satisfy the Master that he has a *primâ facie* ground of defence, an order is made for judgment. It is only applicable to cases in which the writ has been specially indorsed under Order III., rule 6. It has also been now provided by the Rules of November, 1893, that where on a summons under Order XIV. leave is given to defend, the action may, if the Judge or Master is of opinion that no prolonged trial will be necessary, be ordered to be placed in a special list for trial so as to come on to be heard forthwith without any pleadings. (Indermaur's Practice, 64-67.)

Q. What judgments by default is a plaintiff entitled to sign in the following cases respectively by reason of the non-appearance of a defendant :—(1) Writ indorsed for £100, money lent. (2) Writ with a similar indorsement, but dates and items also being given. (3) Writ indorsed with a general claim for damages. (4) Writ indorsed with a claim for recovery of land?

A. (1 and 2) Final judgment, it is of no consequence whether the writ is specially indorsed or not as the action is to recover a fixed liquidated amount. (3) Interlocutory judgment, that is simply that the plaintiff do recover damages. A writ of inquiry must then be issued for the assessment of the damages with a view to signing final judgment. (4) Judgment for recovery of the land. (Indermaur's Practice, 59-62.)

Q. A defendant in an action for damages for breach of contract has no real defence, but desires to put off the day of payment as long as possible. At what stage can the plaintiff obtain judgment?

A. The plaintiff can here, if the defendant does everything to delay him, only obtain judgment by going to trial, for the summary process of Order XIV. is not applicable to such a case.

Q. Under what circumstances can a plaintiff obtain judgment against a defendant without trial?

A. (1) Where the defendant fails to appear to the writ of summons. (2) On an application for judgment on a specially indorsed writ by a summons under Order XIV. (3) Where the defendant, though he has appeared, fails to deliver a statement of defence. (4) The plaintiff may apply for an order for such judgment as he may be entitled to at any stage of the proceedings on admissions in the pleadings. (Indermaur's Practice, 59, 65, 79, 87.)

Q. Explain the nature of the principal pleadings in an action, stating the limits of the time within which they must respectively be delivered and the consequences of non-delivery in each case.

A. They consist now of plain statements on the part of plaintiff and defendant, being divided into paragraphs numbered consecutively, and each paragraph relating as far as may be to a distinct subject matter, and every allegation must be specifically met, a mere general denial not being sufficient. The statement of claim by the plaintiff must be delivered within six weeks from appearance, or, if defendant demands a statement of claim, then within five weeks of such demand. Statement of defence by defendant within ten days of the statement of claim. Statement of reply within 21 days of defence. If the reply does not contain joinder of issue, a rejoinder is put in within four days of reply. If statement of claim not duly delivered, defendant may apply to dismiss the action for want of prosecution. If defence not duly put in, plaintiff may sign judgment, which is final or interlocutory, according to circumstances. If defence contains a counter-claim, the consequence of omission to put in a reply containing defence thereto, is to enable the defendant to move for judgment on his counter-claim. The consequence of not joining issue either in reply or rejoinder, as the case may be, is that, at the end of the proper time, the matters are deemed put in issue. (Indermaur's Practice, Part II., chap. 3.)

Q. *Mention the chief rules of pleading under Order XIX.*

A. Order XIX. deals with pleadings generally, and mentions the different pleadings to be delivered, and goes into various matters in connection with pleadings in detail. Pleadings are to be as brief as possible, divided into separate paragraphs numbered consecutively, and only material facts are to be stated, and not evidence that is relied on. Dates, sums and numbers are to be expressed in figures. Signature of counsel is not necessary. Pleadings are to be printed if they exceed ten folios. All allegations not specifically denied are to be taken to be admitted. Matters presumed by law in a party's favour need not be alleged. Provisions are made for striking out any pleading which may be unnecessary or scandalous. (Indermaur's Practice, 68-73.)

Q. *In an action of Ejectment is it necessary that the defendant should specially plead in detail his title, or what is a sufficient plea upon his part?*

A. No, it is not ordinarily necessary, it being provided

D

that all defences may be raised by a defendant pleading in his defence that he is in possession. If, however, the defendant's defence consists entirely of equitable matter, then he must plead such matter specifically. Thus, if the plaintiff has orally agreed to sell land to the defendant and then sues to eject him, here the defendant, relying on the equitable doctrine of part performance, must plead that matter specifically. (Indermaur's Practice, 88.)

Q. In an action of ejectment by landlord against tenant, can the defendant, under any and what circumstances, dispute the title of the plaintiff to the land in question?

A. The general rule is that a tenant shall not be allowed to dispute his landlord's title, *i.e.*, the tenant cannot dispute the original right of the person through whom he was let into possession; but the tenant may show that the landlord's title has ceased, or been determined, or parted with. And if the tenant was the true owner though out of possession, and he obtained possession through any defective title (except a lease by deed), his possession is by law remitted back to his rightful title and there is no estoppel. And the tenant is of course entitled to set up as a defence that on the true construction of the demise he himself and not his landlord was entitled to possession at the date specified in the claim. (Broom's Commentaries, 837.)

Q. What are the special rules of pleading in cases where executors sue or are sued? How far is an executor liable for causes of action which have accrued against his testator, and mention any statutes which have affected such liability?

A. There are no special rules beyond this—that claims by or against an executor, or administrator, as such, can only be joined with claims by or against him personally, when the personal claims arise with reference to the estate which he represents; and that the beneficiaries need not be made parties. (Indermaur's Practice, 38.) They are liable for his breaches of contracts, but not, at Common Law, for his torts. But they can be sued for his torts to the real or personal property of another committed within six months before his death, provided the action is commenced within six months after they take up the administration (3 & 4 Will. 4, c. 42, sec. 2); and for his torts causing the death of another under 9 & 10 Vict., c. 93.

Q. What are the principal rules with regard to the amendment of pleadings at the instance (1) *of the party pleading;* (2) *of the opposing party?*

A. (1) Very full powers of amendment exist, and the Court or a Judge has power at any stage to allow an amendment. In addition, the plaintiff may once, at any time before the expiration of his time to reply, or where no defence has been delivered within four weeks from the appearance of the defendant who last appeared, amend his statement of claim without leave. And a defendant, who has in his defence pleaded a set-off or counter-claim, may amend it before the expiration of the time for pleading to the reply, or before pleading thereto; or if no reply, then before the expiration of twenty-eight days from the filing of the defence. (2) The Court or a Judge has full power at any stage of the proceedings to order any matter to be struck out which is scandalous, or tends to embarrass or delay the fair trial of the action, and to make all amendments necessary for the purpose of determining the real question in controversy between the parties. (Indermaur's Practice, 85, 86.)

Q. Where a plaintiff amends his statement of claim without leave, what are the rules with regard to the defendant pleading to the amended statement of claim?

A. The defendant should plead to the amended pleading, or amend his pleading, within the balance of the time he then has to plead to the original pleading, or within eight days from the delivery of the amended pleading, whichever may last expire. And if the defendant has already pleaded before the delivery of the amended pleading, and does not plead again or amend within the time just mentioned, he is to be deemed to rely on his original pleading in answer to such amended pleading. (Indermaur's Practice, 86, 87.)

Q. Explain the defences of tender and payment into Court, and their effect upon costs.

A. Tender is a defence set up in an action to the effect that prior to action the party offered the other a certain sum. A tender must be absolute and unconditional, and the person tendering must have been always ready thereafter to pay the money, though the tender was refused. When after a tender the party is sued, he pleads the tender, and pays the amount he tendered into Court, and any plea of tender must always be accompanied by payment into Court. If the plaintiff does not recover more, the defendant gets the costs of the action. Payment into Court is made where the defendant admits the plaintiff's claim to a certain amount. If made unconditionally, the plaintiff may take the money out, and if he accepts it in satisfaction he may get his costs, unless it is paid in with a plea of tender. If he does not accept it in satisfaction, he may still take it out of Court, but the action goes on, and if the plaintiff does not recover more he will not get any costs incurred after the payment in. If it is paid in in the alternative, with a defence denying liability, the plaintiff may accept it in satisfaction, and get his costs, but if he does not do this, he cannot take it out, and the action goes on, and if the plaintiff does not recover more than paid in the defendant will get his costs. (Indermaur's Practice, 95-99.)

Q. State shortly the effect of the rules as to payment of money into Court in an action. In what cases may money be paid in with a denial of liability, and what is the effect of such payment?

A. (1) A defendant in any action for debt or damages may pay money into Court before or with the delivery of his defence, or by leave of the Court or a Judge at any later time, which payment in shall be taken to admit the claim, or cause of action, in respect of which the payment is made. (2) The defendant may also pay money into Court with a defence denying liability, except in actions or counter-claims for libel or slander. When such a payment in is made the plaintiff may accept the amount and tax his costs, but he cannot take it out except in satisfaction. Such payment in does not admit liability, and if the plaintiff does not recover more than so paid in, the defendant gets his costs from the time of payment in. (Indermaur's Practice, 95-99.)

Q. Where payment into Court has been made, either with defence or otherwise, ought this fact to be communicated to the jury?

A. No; it is specially provided that where an action is tried by a Judge with a jury, no communication to the jury is to be made until after the verdict is given, either of the fact that money has been paid into Court, or of the amount paid in; but the jury are to be required to find the amount of the debt or damages, as the case may be, without reference to any payment into Court. (Indermaur's Practice, 99, 100.)

Q. Under what circumstances may an action be brought on for trial without any pleadings?

A. (1) When on a summons under Order XIV., leave being given to defendant, the action is put into the special list for trial (see *ante*, p. 31). (2) A plaintiff may indorse on his writ a statement sufficient to give notice of the nature of his claim and state that if the defendant appears he intends to proceed to trial without pleadings. If the defendant appears, the plaintiff may then, within ten days of appearance, serve 21 days' notice of trial without pleadings. If the defendant is not satisfied to have the action thus disposed of, he may, however, within ten days of appearance, take out a summons for delivery of a statement of claim, and if an order is made the ordinary pleadings take place, or instead of this any necessary particulars may be ordered to be delivered. (Indermaur's Practice, 68, 69.)

Q. Where an action is proceeding to trial without pleadings by reason of the plaintiff's notice to that effect, what defences are open to the defendant at the trial?

A. Subject to any order for particulars, all defences are open to the defendant—except that if he has not taken out a summons for delivery of a statement of claim, he cannot rely on a set-off or counter-claim, or on the defences of infancy, coverture, fraud, Statutes of Limitation, or discharge under the Bankruptcy Acts, unless he has within ten days after appearance given notice to the plaintiff stating the grounds and particulars upon which he relies. (Indermaur's Practice, 69.)

3.—INTERLOCUTORY PROCEEDINGS.

Q. Enumerate some of the various interlocutory applications that may be made during an action.

A. Summonses may be according to circumstances taken out for any of the following matters: (1) For time to deliver pleadings; (2) For particulars of claim or defence; (3) For leave to administer interrogatories; (4) For the opponent to make an affidavit of documents; (5) For the action to be transferred to the County Court; (6) To change the place of trial; (7) For the plaintiff to be ordered to give security for costs; (8) To refer the action to a referee or arbitrator. (Indermaur's Practice, Part II., chap. 4.)

Q. Must separate summonses be taken out for every particular thing which is required in the course of an action, or may several applications be embodied in one summons?

A. Separate individual applications may be made, or one general Summons for Directions may be taken out in the Queen's Bench Division, though not in the Chancery Division. A Summons for Directions may embody generally all things required. It must be served not less than four days before the return day, and on the hearing of such summons, any party, as far as practicable, should apply for any order or directions as to any interlocutory matter or thing that he may require. A Summons for Directions having once been taken out, any application subsequently for any directions as to any interlocutory matter is made under the original summons by giving two clear days' notice to the other party stating the grounds of the application, and thus the issue of any fresh summons is avoided. (Indermaur's Practice, 91, 92.)

Q. What is meant by discovery? How many kinds of discovery are there?

A. Obtaining from the opposite party to the litigation knowledge of documents and facts. There are two kinds of discovery, viz.: (1) Of facts by means of interrogatories, and (2) of documents by means of an affidavit of documents and inspection thereof on notice or order. (Indermaur's Practice, 100, 102.)

Q. By what proceedings can one party to an action compel his opponent to disclose facts or documents? Describe the practice relating to such proceedings.

A. As to facts, interrogatories may be administered, but leave must first be obtained. The interrogatories must be answered on oath within ten days. £5 has to be paid into Court to security for costs account before delivery, and if the interrogatories exceed five folios 10s. for every additional folio. As to documents, a summons may be taken out asking that the opponent makes an affidavit stating what documents he has in his possession, custody, or power. Here also £5 has to be paid into Court, and such amount may under special circumstances be increased. (Indermaur's Practice, 100, 106.)

Q. State the principal rules for obtaining discovery and inspection of documents.

A. Discovery of documents may be obtained by either

party to an action by summons, unsupported by affidavit, asking for an order for his opponent to make an affidavit of documents. Before an order can be made £5 must be paid into Court to the "security for costs account," as an indemnity in respect of the costs of the discovery, unless for special reasons this is dispensed with by the Court, and such amount may under special circumstances be increased. Inspection is usually obtained by giving notice to produce documents enumerated in any affidavit or pleading, when the other party should, within two days, if the documents are all specified in an affidavit of documents, or within four days if specified otherwise, deliver a notice stating a time within three days, at which they may be inspected at his solicitor's office. If the notice above referred to is not complied with, the documents generally cannot be given in evidence, but the party has also a right to compel inspection by taking out a summons. In addition to this, in the first instance, a summons for inspection may be taken out, but if so, it must be supported by affidavit showing (1) of what documents inspection is sought; (2) that the party applying is entitled to inspect; (3) that they are in the possession or power of the other party. (Indermaur's Practice, 102-105.)

Q. Upon what subjects, and within what limits, may one party to an action administer interrogatories to his opponent?

A. Interrogatories may be administered as regards all relevant facts tending to support the interrogating party's case, but they must not be mere "fishing" questions. In all cases, however, leave must first be obtained on summons for the delivery of the interrogatories. Improper questions may be struck out on the application of the party interrogated. Before delivery of the interrogatories, there must be paid into Court by the interrogating party to the "security for costs account" a sum of £5, and if the interrogatories exceed five folios in length, the further sum of 10s. for every additional folio. (Indermaur's Practice, 107, 108.)

Q. In what cases will a plaintiff be compelled to give security for costs ?

A. (1) When the plaintiff is permanently resident abroad, even though temporarily here, unless, indeed, he has substantial property here. (2) To a limited extent, in action of tort under the provisions of the County Courts Act 1888 (sec. 66), for here if defendant can show by affidavit that the plaintiff has no visible means of paying costs if the verdict goes against him, an order will be made for security, or that the action be transferred to the County Court, unless the plaintiff can satisfy the Judge that he has a cause of action fit to be prosecuted in the superior Court. (3) When the trustee of a bankrupt plaintiff continues an action commenced by the bankrupt. (4) When a limited joint stock company is plaintiff, if it can be shewn that their assets may be insufficient to pay costs. There are also some other cases, but the above are the chief. (Indermaur's Practice, 115-118.)

Q. A foreigner residing out of the jurisdiction being sued, puts forward a counter-claim. Can he be called upon to give security for costs ?

A. He cannot be called upon to give security for the costs of the action, but he can for the costs of the counter-claim, if it is strictly a counter-claim as distinguished from set-off (see *ante*, p. 29), for this constitutes a distinct cause of action against the plaintiff. (Lake v. Haseltine, 55 L. J., Q. B., 205 ; Indermaur's Practice, 116.)

Q. Under what circumstances, and how, can an action of tort brought in the High Court be remitted to the County Court ?

A. Under the County Courts Act 1888 (sec 66), if the defendant can shew by affidavit that the plaintiff has no visible means of paying costs if the verdict goes against him, an order will be made for the plaintiff to give security, or that the action be transferred to the County Court, unless the plaintiff can satisfy the Judge that he has a cause of

action fit to be prosecuted in the High Court. (Indermaur's
Practice, 116, 117.)

*Q. In what cases can a defendant in an action who is
about to leave the country be arrested and imprisoned on
mesne process? For how long can he be so imprisoned? What
effect has the signing of final judgment in the action upon the
imprisonment?*

A. When the plaintiff can prove that the defendant is
indebted to him in the amount of £50, and that his absence
from England will prejudice him in the prosecution of his
action, he may obtain an order for the defendant to be
arrested for a period not exceeding six months, unless and
until he gives security that he will not go abroad. In an
action for a penalty under some statute the plaintiff need
not, however, prove that the defendant's absence will so
prejudice him, and in this case the security is for the debt.
The defendant cannot be kept in prison after final judgment
has been signed. (Indermaur's Practice, 112, 113.)

*Q. What means exist for enabling a party to attain
evidence before trial?*

A. If in any case it happens that a person who will be
required as a witness at the trial is about to go abroad, or is
very old, or is so ill that he is in danger of death, an order
may be obtained for the taking of his evidence *de bene esse.*
Such an application must be supported by affidavit, showing
that the person's evidence is material, and that he is about to
go abroad, or is very old, or is dangerously ill; and in the
last case there must be an affidavit by a medical man. The
evidence so obtained can (except by consent) only be used
if it is shown to the satisfaction of the Judge at the trial
that the deponent is unable to attend. (Indermaur's
Practice, 136, 137.)

*Q. What is a " Special Case," and what is the course of
procedure thereon?*

A. It is a means resorted to (a) by consent, where the

parties are agreed on the facts, and only require the decision of the Court on a point of law; and (b) where the Court or a Judge directs one to be stated for the purpose of obtaining a decision on a point of law. The special case is entered for argument, and comes on in due course to be heard. The parties to a special case may agree that on the determination of the point in dispute, a certain sum shall be paid by the one to the other, either with or without costs, and the judgment of the Court may be given therefor and execution issued thereon. (Indermaur's Practice, 121, 122.)

Q. What are the existing provisions for referring an action or any issues therein instead of allowing the same to proceed and be disposed of in the ordinary manner?

A. Under the Arbitration Act 1889, a Judge may at any time refer any question for inquiry and report to an official or special referee. It is also provided that (1) if all the parties interested who are not under disability consent, *or* (2) if the matter requires any prolonged examination of documents or any scientific or local investigation which cannot in the opinion of the Judge be conveniently disposed of in the ordinary manner, *or* (3) if the question in dispute consists wholly or in part of matters of account, the Judge may at any time order the whole cause or matter or any question or issue of fact therein to be tried before a special referee or arbitrator, agreed on by the parties, or before an official referee or officer of the Court. (Indermaur's Practice, 176, 177.)

Q. Is there any appeal from either a Master's or a Judge's decision on an interlocutory application in Chambers?

A. Yes, any party affected by a Master's order may appeal to a Judge in Chambers (either by a written notice or an indorsement on the summons) within four days, and from a Judge in Chambers an appeal may be made to the Divisional Court within eight days. The appeal notice must in each case be returnable within these times. Any such appeal is no stay of proceedings unless so ordered. (Indermaur's Practice, 123, 124.)

Q. What are the provisions of the Judicature Acts for (1) *discontinuing an action;* (2) *dismissing an action for want of prosecution;* (3) *abandoning any part of a statement of claim or defence?*

A. (1) Plaintiff may discontinue the action at any time before receipt of the statement of defence, or after delivery of the statement of defence, if he has taken no proceedings other than an interlocutory application, by giving a notice in writing to the defendant, and paying the defendant's costs. He cannot discontinue the action at any other stage of the proceedings without leave of a Court or a Judge. (Indermaur's Practice, 124.) (2) The defendant may apply to dismiss the action for want of prosecution when the plaintiff omits within due time:—(*a*) To deliver his statement of claim. (*b*) To obey an order for discovery. (*c*) To give notice of trial. (*Ib.*, 112.) (3) Abandonment of any part of a pleading can only be made by leave of a Court or Judge, except in cases in which amendments are allowed without leave.

4.—TRIAL AND SUBSEQUENT PROCEEDINGS.

Q. What are the different modes of trial of an action? Give the substance of the principal rules now in force with reference to determining the mode to be adopted.

A. (1) Before a Judge with a jury. In actions of libel, slander, false imprisonment, malicious prosecution, seduction, and breach of promise of marriage, either plaintiff or defendant may have a jury as of right; but in all other actions notice of trial before a jury cannot be given, though an order can be obtained for that purpose on application of either party, within ten days after notice of trial given. (2) Before a Judge without a jury. Except in the six actions named above, the trial is *primâ facie* in this way. (3) Before an official or special referee. This can only be by order. (4) Before a Judge, or official, or special referee, with assessors. This can only be by order. (Indermaur's Practice, 127-129.)

Q. Under what circumstances, if any, can a plaintiff claim the right to have his case tried by a jury (1) in the High Court; (2) in a County Court?

A. (1) In actions of libel, slander, seduction, false imprisonment, malicious prosecution, and breach of promise of marriage, the plaintiff may give notice for trial by Judge and jury; and if he gives notice for trial by a Judge without a jury, the defendant may, within four days after service of notice of trial, obtain a jury by merely giving notice for one. In other cases, notice cannot be given for trial by a jury, but on application of either party, within ten days after notice of trial, an order will be made for a jury. (Indermaur's Practice, 128.) (2) If the amount claimed exceeds £5, either party has a right to a jury; but in other cases, a jury can only be obtained by leave.

Q. At what stage of an action should notice of trial be given, and what length of notice is necessary?

A. In all actions in which there are pleadings, the notice of trial must be given within six weeks of the close of the pleadings, otherwise the defendant may apply to dismiss the action for want of prosecution. Ten days' notice is necessary unless the defendant is under terms to take short notice, which means four days. If the plaintiff has indorsed on his writ a notice that he intends to proceed to trial without pleadings, and the action is so proceeding, 21 days' notice of trial must be given within ten days of appearance. (Indermaur's Practice, 127.)

Q. By whom are jurors summoned? Distinguish between the functions and qualifications of jurors in early days of English history and at the present time.

Can either party to an action take any objection, and how, to the jurors?

A. By the sheriff. Formerly, jurors were witnesses who were chosen because they knew and could testify of the facts in issue; now, a common juror must not be a witness, must be over 21 and under 60, and must have £10 a year in freeholds or copyholds, or £20 a year in leaseholds, or be rated to the poor at £30 in Middlesex or £20 elsewhere. Either party may challenge the array (*i.e.*, the whole panel) or the polls (*i.e.*, individual jurors), for cause shown. (Indermaur's Practice, 137, note (*g*)).

Q. Describe the order of proceedings upon a trial by jury, distinguishing the province of the Judge from that of the jury.

A. The counsel for the party on whom the affirmative rests is ordinarily entitled to begin at the trial. He states shortly the effect of the pleadings, states his client's case, and proceeds to call his witnesses. These are examined by him, cross-examined by the opposing counsel, and re-examined if necessary. The case being closed, the opposing counsel opens his case to the jury, and his witnesses are examined, cross-examined, and re-examined, and the opposing counsel then addresses the jury, the counsel for the party commencing having the right to reply. If the opposing counsel calls no witnesses, and puts in no documentary evidence, then the counsel who began must, at the close of his case, address the jury, and the opposing counsel thus gets the last word to the jury. The Judge then sums up, and the jury consider, and give their verdict. It is for the Judge to direct the jury on all points of law, and for the jury to find the facts. After the verdict it is for the Judge to pronounce the proper judgment, and no motion for judgment is now necessary. (Indermaur's Practice, 139, 143.)

Q. What are the chief functions of a Judge on a trial at nisi prius?

A. He has to preside at the trial and to determine on

the admissibility or inadmissibility of evidence tendered, also to check any irrelevant or improper examination or cross-examination. He should protect a witness from answering questions which may tend to criminate him. He explains any points occurring on which the jury require assistance. He sums up the case to the jury, and directs them on the law, and on the points as to which their verdict is required. After verdict he gives judgment, and, if necessary, considers and decides on the matter of costs.

Q. What is the effect of giving (1) *notice to admit documents at the trial of an action;* (2) *notice to produce documents at the trial ?*

A. (1) The effect is that if the party to whom the notice is given admits the documents they are then admissible, and if he does not, then the costs of proving them have to be borne by him, unless at the trial the Judge certifies that the refusal to admit was reasonable. No costs of proving any document are allowed when such notice has not been given, unless in the opinion of the Taxing Master the omission to give the notice has been a saving of expense. (2) The effect of giving notice to produce is that if the party to whom the notice is given has the documents in his possession and fails to produce them, secondary evidence of them may be admitted. (Indermaur's Practice, 131, 132.)

Q. What are the proper steps to take in preparing evidence for trial?

A. Ordinarily *subpœnas* are issued for the witnesses to attend the trial to give evidence *vivâ voce*, but by consent the evidence may be by affidavit, or the Court may order any particular fact to be proved by affidavit. Practically, however, evidence is never taken by affidavit in the Queen's Bench Division, though it is sometimes in the Chancery Division. It is usual to see the witnesses beforehand, and prepare their proofs, that is take notes of the facts they can prove. Notice to produce any original documents in the opponent's possession should be given, and, as regards documents in a party's own possession, a notice to inspect and admit should be given. (Indermaur's Practice, 131-136.)

Q. What are the rules ordinarily observed at a trial with regard to (1) the examination of witnesses; (2) the proof of attested deeds?

A. (1) The party whose witnesses they are examines them in the first instance, and in doing so he must be careful not to ask leading questions, unless, indeed, they are in the opinion of the Judge adverse witnesses. After examination the opposing party cross-examines, and then the other party has a right to re-examine on matters arising out of the cross-examination. If in the opinion of the Judge a witness is adverse, the party calling him may contradict him by other evidence, or by leave of the Judge may show he made a previous contrary statement, the circumstances thereof being first mentioned to him. (2) If attestation was necessary to the validity of the instrument, the attesting witness must be called, or if dead, evidence of his handwriting given. If attestation was not necessary, other proof may be given, *e.g.*, by calling a person who saw the instrument executed though he did not attest, or by calling a person who knows the handwriting, or by admission, or even by comparison of handwriting. (Indermaur's Principles of Common Law, 460, 463, 464.)

Q. Describe the process for obtaining the attendance of witnesses at a trial. If a witness, duly summoned, fails to attend, to what consequences is he liable?

A. The ordinary course is by a *subpœna ad testificandum*, but if the witness is required to bring documents with him a *subpœna duces tecum*. A witness resident in Scotland or Ireland can only be subpœnaed by leave. If a witness is abroad, a commission may be issued, and, if in the Colonies, a mandamus to the Court there to examine, or in any case a request to the foreign Court to examine. If a witness is in custody on civil process his evidence is obtained by *habeas corpus ad testificandum*, and if on criminal process by an order from one of the principal Secretaries of State or a Judge at Chambers. (Indermaur's Practice, 135, 136.) If a witness has been duly subpœnaed, and proper conduct money paid, and he does not attend, he is liable to a penalty of £10, and he is also liable to an action for damages. (Indermaur's Principles of Common Law, 444.)

Q. *What is meant by and what are the consequences of (1) a special verdict, (2) a non-suit, and (3) a withdrawal of a juror respectively?*

A. (1) A special verdict is one not merely for the plaintiff or for the defendant, but on such questions as the Judge has thought fit to leave to the jury. It is the duty of the Judge to direct such judgment to be entered as he thinks right. (2) A non-suit is technically where the plaintiff does not appear at the trial, but it more usually occurs where the plaintiff does practically appear, but the Judge considers he has no case, and at once decides against him without letting the matter go to the jury. In such a case the rule still appears to be that the action may be brought over again. (3) This means that the parties come to terms, and the effect of a juror being withdrawn is that the action is at an end, and each party pays his own costs. (Indermaur's Practice, 140-143.)

Q. *Define a judgment* quando acciderint, *and state under what circumstances, and how, such judgment is enforced.*

A. It is a judgment against an executor or administrator in respect of assets which may thereafter come to his hands. When an executor or administrator pleads *plene administravit*, or *plene administravit præter*, and the plaintiff cannot disprove that plea, he should sign such a judgment. It is enforced thus :—When the plaintiff knows that assets have come to the defendant's hands he should serve a demand for payment, and on failure to comply with this, he should take out a summons for liberty to issue execution, and on proof that the defendant has so acquired assets an order will be made. (Indermaur's Practice, 163.)

Q. Under what circumstances will a new trial be granted when a cause has been tried and a verdict pronounced by a jury? To what Court must an application for a new trial be now made?

A. When either party is dissatisfied with the verdict on any of the following grounds:—(1) Misdirection by the Judge, or improper omission or rejection of evidence, but this will only succeed when the Court is of opinion some substantial wrong has been occasioned; (2) That the Judge was disqualified by reason of pecuniary interest; (3) That the successful party, or an officer of the Court or the jury were guilty of gross misconduct; (4) That the damages are grossly excessive or utterly inadequate; (5) Surprise; (6) That new evidence has been discovered; (7) That the verdict was obtained by perjury and conspiracy; (8) That the verdict was manifestly against the weight of evidence. The application must now in all cases be made to the Court of Appeal. (Indermaur's Practice, 145, 146.)

Q. Explain the modes of enforcing judgment in an action.

A. (1) *Fieri facias* for the seizing and selling the debtor's goods. (2) *Capias ad satisfaciendum* for the taking of the body subject to the Debtors Act 1869, and also a judgment summons under that Act. (3) *Elegit* for the seizing lands; and, if the debtor has only an equitable estate, or, indeed, any property which cannot be seized in execution in the ordinary manner, by the appointment of a receiver, which is called equitable execution. (4) Garnishee order for attaching and obtaining debts due to the judgment debtor. (5) Charging order to obtain payment out of stock of the judgment debtor. (6) Writ for the delivery up of certain property. (7) Writ of possession for the putting of a person in possession of lands for the recovery of which he has a judgment. (8) Writ of sequestration for levying on a person's property to compel obedience to the judgment. (9) Writ of attachment under which the party may be committed to prison. (10) Writs of *ji. fa. de bonis ecclesiasticis,* and *sequestrari facias* for raising the amount of the judgment out of the benefice of the defendant, who is a clergyman. (Indermaur's Practice, 149-161.)

Q. What is the form of the writ of fieri facias, *and what effects of the debtor are exempted from its operation?*

A. It is a writ directed to the sheriff commanding him to seize and sell sufficient of the judgment debtor's goods to satisfy the judgment. (Indermaur's Practice, 149.) The following are some of the chief things exempted from being taken under such a writ :—(1) Wearing apparel and bedding and implements of trade of any judgment debtor not exceeding £5. (2) Goods of a stranger. (3) Goods in *custodia legis.* (4) Fixtures. (Notes to Simpson v. Hartopp, Indermaur's Common Law Cases, 17.)

Q. What is a "garnishee order"? State the principal provisions of the existing law as to the attachment of debts.

A. A garnishee order is an order obtained by a judgment creditor against a third person to pay to him money owing by such third person to the judgment debtor. It is obtained in the first instance *ex parte,* on affidavit by the judgment creditor or his solicitor, of judgment having been recovered and being still unsatisfied, and of a debt being due from some third person within the jurisdiction. On this an order is made for the third person to attend and show cause why he should not pay the debt to the judgment creditor. Unless good cause is shown, the order is made absolute, and then enforced by execution. If the plaintiff does not know any one owing money to the judgment

debtor, he may obtain an order for the debtor to attend and
be orally examined as to what debts are owing to him. A
garnishee order cannot be obtained against wages owing to
any seaman, servant, labourer, or workman. (Indermaur's
Practice, 156, 157.)

*Q. State the general rules as to costs on trial of an
action.*

A. Under the provisions of the Judicature Act 1890, and
of Order LXV., rule 1, costs are in the discretion of the
Court or Judge, subject to this, that when an action is tried
by a jury costs follow the event, unless for good cause shewn
otherwise ordered. By reason of the County Courts Act
1888 (51 & 52 Vict., c. 43, sec. 116), if the plaintiff recovers
less than £20 on contract, or £10 on tort, he gets no costs
without a special certificate or order, and if, though recovering these amounts respectively, he recovers not exceeding
£50 on contract (Millington v. Harwood (1892), Q. B., 166)
or less than £20 on tort, he only gets costs on the County
Court scale unless otherwise ordered. But these provisions
have no application where the action is one which could not
have been commenced in the County Court, and here,
however small an amount the plaintiff recovers, he gets
his costs unless the Judge otherwise orders. (Garnett v.
Bradley, L. R., 3 H. L., 944; Indermaur's Practice,
165-167.)

*Q. Can a party who has succeeded in an action be made
to pay the costs of his opponent ? Does any appeal lie on a
question of costs?*

A. Yes, for costs are in the Judge's discretion, and though
in a trial by jury they follow the event, this is only if there
is no contrary order. It has, however, been decided that
it is not within the discretion of the Court to make a
defendant pay the whole costs of the action if the plaintiff
had no right to sue. There is no appeal on a question of
costs only, but this does not apply where a Judge exceeds

his jurisdiction. Thus, if a plaintiff has no right of action and the defendant wholly succeeds, but the Judge nevertheless orders the defendant to pay the plaintiff's costs, an appeal would lie. (Indermaur's Practice, 169, 170.)

Q. What is the time allowed for appealing, and how and to what tribunal is the appeal brought from the decision of a divisional Court?

A. To the Court of Appeal, within three months if it is a final judgment or order, or if it is an interlocutory order, within 14 days, by notice of motion. The time within which to appeal to the Court of Appeal is calculated from the time at which the judgment or order was signed, entered, or otherwise perfected, or in the case of the refusal of an application, from the date of such refusal. Where an *ex parte* application to a Divisional Court has been made and refused, an application to the Court of Appeal for a similar purpose must be made within four days. (Indermaur's Practice, 269, 270.)

Q. How is an appeal to the Court of Appeal brought, and with what powers and duties is the Court of Appeal clothed when dealing with an appeal from the Court of First Instance?

A. An appeal to the Court of Appeal is brought on by means of a notice of motion, stating whether the whole or part only (and what part) of the judgment or order appealed from is complained of. The notice is a 14 days' notice if from a final judgment or order, and four days' notice if from an interlocutory order, and must be served on all parties directly affected by the appeal. The Court has all powers and duties as to amendment and otherwise of the Court of First Instance, with full power to receive further evidence on questions of fact orally or by affidavit. The Court may draw inferences of fact, and give any judgment, and make any order which ought to have been made, and has full power over costs. (Indermaur's Practice, 270-273.)

5.—MISCELLANEOUS.

Q. What is (1) *a writ of mandamus;* (2) *injunction;* (3) *a writ of certiorari; and in what cases are they respectively issued?*

A. (1) Writs of mandamus are of two sorts. One is a prerogative writ issued out of the Queen's Bench requiring some inferior Court to do some particular thing appertaining to its office and duty, and is confined to cases of infringement of some public right or duty, where no effectual relief can be obtained by an ordinary action at law. An instance of the writ occurs where a justice is required to do some act relating to his office. The second writ of mandamus is under the Common Law Procedure Act 1854, to compel the performance of any duty in the fulfilment of which the plaintiff is personally interested. (2) An injunction is an order of the Court prohibiting the doing of a certain act, or commanding its doing, in which case it is called a mandatory injunction. (3) A writ of certiorari is a writ issued for the purpose of removing any matter, or cause, from some inferior Court into the Queen's Bench Division, on the ground that a partial or insufficient trial only will be had below. (Broom's Commentaries, 209, 212, 219.)

Q. What is a writ of attachment, and how and under what circumstances may it be obtained? Can imprisonment for debt be now enforced?

A. A writ of attachment is a process from the Court whereby a person is committed to prison for contempt of Court. It is used as a means of enforcing the doing of specific acts ordered by the Court. It is obtained by motion, of which notice has to be duly served, stating in general terms the grounds of the application, and a copy of any affidavit intended to be used on the motion must be served with the notice. (Indermaur's Practice, 237, 238.) Imprisonment for debt is still allowed under the Debtors Act 1869

(32 & 33 Vict., c. 62) in the following cases:—(1) Where default is made in payment of a penalty other than a penalty on a contract; (2) where default is made in payment of a sum recoverable summarily before justices; (3) where default is made by a trustee or other person in a fiduciary capacity in obeying an order to pay over money in his possession; (4) where default is made by a solicitor in payment of costs ordered to be paid for misconduct, or in payment of money ordered to be paid in his character of an officer of the Court; (5) where default is made by a bankrupt in paying over for the benefit of his creditors a portion of salary or other income which he has been ordered to pay; (6) where default is made in payment of sums in respect of the payment of which orders are by that Act authorised to be made. With regard to the cases numbered 3 and 4 it is, however, now provided by 41 & 42 Vict., c. 54, that the Court has a discretion as to imprisoning. The imprisonment must not exceed one year. Also, under the Debtors Act 1869, a judgment debtor can be imprisoned for not more than six weeks on proof of means to pay. (Indermaur's Common Law, 357-359.)

Q. Describe the object of, and the procedure upon, the writs of mandamus, prohibition, and certiorari respectively.

A. (a) The object of a writ of mandamus is to enforce the performance by any person, corporation, or inferior Court of some specified duty which the Court deems consonant with right and justice. To obtain the writ, application must be made by motion to the Queen's Bench Division, supported by affidavit, showing that the applicant has a right to have something done, and has no other specific means of compelling its performance. On service of the writ, the mandatory must comply with it, or make a return showing why he does not do so, and unless he complies or succeeds in quashing the writ as insufficient on its face, he must answer or demur ; if judgment goes against him, the Court awards a peremptory mandamus with, in cases of private injury, damages and costs. (b) Prohibition lies from a superior Court to an inferior one which attempts to exceed its jurisdiction. The application is made by summons or motion, supported by affidavit showing the facts and the excess of jurisdiction. (c) Certiorari lies for the removal of proceedings into the High Court of Justice from any inferior Court before judgment; the writ is sued out and left with the proper officer of the inferior Court; all proceedings are stayed in the inferior Court, and the record itself is returned into the High Court to be preceeded on there. (Broom's Commentaries, 209, 216, 219.)

Q. *Explain the meaning of and procedure with regard to* (1) *a petition of right,* (2) *a writ of habeas corpus.*

A. (1) A petition of right is an extraordinary mode of redress at the suit of a subject against the Crown, claiming any hereditament or chattel. There is first the petition, and then on answer indorsed thereon by the sovereign, *soit droit fait al partie,* a commission is issued to enquire into the matter. After the return of the commission, the Attorney-General may plead in bar, and the question raised is determined upon issue or demurrer. (Broom's Commentaries, 234.) (2) This is a writ to effect deliverance from illegal confinement, existing at Common Law, and amended and perpetuated by various statutes, the chief of which is known as the Habeas Corpus Act (31 Car. 2, c. 2). The writ is granted on motion out of the Queen's Bench Division. The return is made by producing the prisoner, and setting forth the grounds and proceedings upon which he is in custody, and then the matter is argued. If the return is deemed to present sufficient matter in justification of the prisoner's detention, he is remanded to his former custody ; if insufficient he is discharged therefrom. (Broom's Commentaries, 229.)

Q. (a) *Explain the procedure in interpleader.* (b) *Can an auctioneer, who sells goods under instructions from A, with an indemnity from him obtained after notice of a claim by B, avail himself of the procedure of interpleader when sued for the proceeds of the sale?*

A. (*a*) Issue a summons calling the two claimants before a Judge; the applicant must support his summons by an affidavit that (1) he claims no interest in the subject matter other than for charges or costs; (2) he does not collude with any of the claimants; and (3) he is willing to pay or transfer the subject matter into Court, or dispose of it as the Court or a Judge may direct; the Judge hears the application, and makes an order upon it, usually directing an issue to be tried between the two claimants, and if the amount involved does not exceed £500, such issue may be tried in the County Court. (Indermaur's Practice, 119, 120.) (*b*) Yes, he can do so (Thompson & Wright, 54 L. J., Q. B., 32); but it would be otherwise if he had identified himself with one of the claimants (Tucker v. Morris, 2 L. J., Ex., 1), or had colluded with either of them.

Q. Explain the meaning of and describe the practice in replevin.

A. Replevin is a course that may be taken by a person whose goods have been wrongfully seized by another, *e.g.*, in distress. A replevin bond is entered into before the registrar of the district County Court, with two sureties; an action is then commenced to try the question of the right to the goods. In the meantime the goods remain in the possession of the party on whom the distress, &c., has been levied; and if the matter is determined against him he has to give them up. (Indermaur's Practice, 58, note (*q*).)

Q. Give instances in which a wrong may be redressed by the act of the party injured without recourse to legal proceedings by way of action.

A. (1) Self-defence, by which a man may use force to

repel force as regards himself, his wife, child, servant, or friend, and his goods. (2) Recaption or reprisal, which allows a man to retake his goods peaceably from any one who has wrongfully taken possession of them. (3) Entry on lands, by which a person may peaceably resume possession of his own lands as against a wrongful holder. (4) Abatement, which enables a man to put a stop to a nuisance peaceably. (5) Distress, which allows a man to seize the goods of his tenant for rent in arrear, or the cattle of another *damage feasant.* (6) Seizure of heriots when due.

Q. Can a lawful owner of a house of which another is in wrongful possession repossess himself by entry without obtaining judgment in ejectment? What is the effect of a forcible entry? State and discuss the decision in Newton v. Harland.

A. There is considerable conflict of judicial authority on this point. The Statute 5 Rich. 2, c. 1, prohibits any forcible entry. In Newton v. Harland (1 M. & Gr., 644) it was held that a forcible entry, being unlawful under the statute, could not give such lawful possession as would enable the owner to justify the forcible expulsion of the wrongful holder. Any party so entering is clearly liable to be indicted under the statute, and it seems that the wrongful holder may obtain damages, not for the forcible entry, but in respect of any wrongful independent acts which are done in the course of or after the forcible entry. (Indermaur's Principles of Common Law, 312.)

Q. Discuss the question how far an agreement ousting the jurisdiction of our Courts is enforceable or void.

A. Such an agreement is void on the ground of public policy. It is, however, lawful to enter into an agreement as to the mode of settling the amount of damage or the time for payment or any similar matter which does not go to the root of the action. The question whether an arbitration is necessary before a complete cause of action arises, or whether the agreement to refer disputes is collateral and independent, must be determined by the construction of the particular contract, and the intention of the parties collected from its language. Where there is an agreement to do a thing, and to refer any dispute in connection therewith to arbitration, and one party sues upon a breach of the agreement, the other may at any time after appearance, and before taking any other step in the action, apply to a Judge at Chambers to stay the action, on the ground that he is and always has been ready to proceed with the submission to arbitration, and that there is no sufficient reason why it should not thus be proceeded with. (Arbitration Act 1889, sec. 4; Indermaur's Practice, 178, 179.)

Q. Define the jurisdiction of the County Court in actions of tort and of contract. Can a plaintiff, and if so by what means, commence an action in the County Court where his demand is for a sum in excess of the jurisdiction of the Court?

A. The County Court has a general jurisdiction, both in tort and contract, up to £50, except in libel, slander, breach of promise of marriage, and seduction. The plaintiff can abandon the excess, and thus bring the case in the County Court, or under section 64 of the County Courts Act 1888, it may be brought in the County Court for the full amount by consent signed by both parties or their solicitors.

Q. What are the limits of jurisdiction of a County Court in an action of contract? Explain the meaning of the enactment against splitting demands in those Courts.

A. All actions of contract except breach of promise to marry, if the claim is not more than £50, whether on balance of account or otherwise, may be commenced in the County Court (County Courts Act 1888, sec. 56), or by signed consent, any action that can be brought in the Queen's Bench Division (*Ib.*, sec. 64). The plaintiff may not divide his cause of action where it exceeds £50 for the

purpose of bringing two or more actions in the County Court,
but may abandon the excess above £50 (*Ib.*, sec. 81).

*Q. How is an action in the County Court commenced?
What are the proceedings upon a default summons, and in what
cases can such a summons be issued?*

A. It is commenced by plaint, which must be entered in
the County Court within the district of which the defendant,
or one of the defendants, resides or carries on business,
except in certain cases by leave. The default summons must
be personally served, and if no notice of intention to defend
is given within eight days of service, the plaintiff may sign
judgment. Such a summons may be issued where the action
is for a debt or liquidated money demand. (County Courts
Act 1888.)

*Q. What is the jurisdiction of a County Court in cases of
ejectment, or where questions of title to land are involved?
How is the defendant to avail himself of the want of jurisdiction?*

A. By the County Courts Act 1888, the jurisdiction
extends to cases where neither the yearly value nor rent
exceed £50; but the defendant or his landlord, within one
month after he is served with the summons, may apply to a
Judge of the High Court in Chambers for a summons for the
plaintiff to shew cause why the action should not be tried in
the High Court on the ground that the title to land of greater
value than £50 a year is affected, and the Judge may order
the action to be tried in the High Court.

*Q. By what process, and on what terms, can an action
be removed from a County Court into the High Court of
Justice?*

A. The mode of removing a cause from the County Court
to the High Court is by writ of certiorari. The right of so
removing a cause exists at Common Law, and now, under
the County Courts Act 1888 (sec. 126), it is provided that it
shall be lawful for the High Court, or a Judge thereof, to

order the removal into the High Court by writ of certiorari or otherwise, of any action or matter commenced in the Court under the provisions of this Act, if the High Court, or a Judge thereof, shall deem it desirable that the action or matter shall be tried in the High Court, and upon such terms as to payment of costs, giving security, or otherwise as the High Court, or a Judge thereof, shall think fit to impose.

Q. How, and under what circumstances, and to what Court or Courts, can an appeal be brought against a decision in a County Court?

A. An appeal may be brought to a Divisional Court of the High Court when the claim is for £20 or upwards, or where leave is given, on the ground of some point of law being wrongly decided, or upon the ground of wrongful admission or rejection of evidence, or in a claim in which the title to corporeal or incorporeal hereditaments is involved. The appeal is now, in all cases, by an eight days' notice of motion within twenty-one days of the decision complained of. (Indermaur's Practice, 281, 282.)

EVIDENCE.

I.—TEST QUESTIONS ON STEPHEN'S DIGEST OF EVIDENCE. 5TH EDITION.

(The numbers at the end of the questions refer to the pages of Stephen's Digest of the Law of Evidence.)

1. What is meant by oral evidence? and by documentary evidence? (2.)

2. What is the difference between conclusive proof and a presumption? (2.)

3. When are facts said to be (1) in issue, (2) relevant? (2.)

4. Of what facts may evidence be given? (3.)

5. If A is tried for cutting B's throat, is a statement made by B (deceased) on running out of the room where A was, but not in A's presence, admissible? (5.)

6. On a trial of A, B and C for conspiracy, are (1) the acts of each, (2) the statements of each, admissible in evidence? (6.)

7. If A and B are charged with conspiracy to defraud the Customs, is (1) an entry by A in a book, (2) an entry by A on the counterfoil of his cheque book, evidence against B? (7).

8. Is evidence to be rejected because it is indecent, or offensive to public morals, or injurious to the feelings of third persons? (156, 157.)

9. If the fact that A did a certain thing (*e.g.*, murdered B) is in issue, can evidence be given to show (1) that A had a motive for doing such a thing, or (2) made preparations for it, or (3) subsequently did acts which a person who had done such a thing would be likely to do? (10, 11.)

10. What do you understand by a statement forming part of the *res gestae*? (158).

11. Would letters written by A be admissible in support of a contention that A had gone abroad with intent to defeat his creditors? (11.)

12. In criminal cases, can evidence be given that the prosecutrix made a complaint against the accused? If so, are the terms of the complaint admissible? (12, 159.)

13. Explain the maxim, *Res inter alios acta alteri nocere non debet*. (159; also see Broom's Maxims.)

14. On an issue whether a brewer supplied good beer to a publican, is evidence admissible to prove the brewer supplied good beer to other publicans? (14.)

15. B's dog bites A, who sues for damages. Is evidence admissible that the dog had previously bitten persons who had complained to B? (17.)

16. Upon the issue whether A said or did something, when is evidence admissible to prove that A said or did a similar thing on another occasion? (15.)

17. How may guilty knowledge of an alleged receiver of stolen goods be proved? (15.)

18. On the question whether a false entry in a book was made intentionally or accidentally by A's servant, is evidence admitted to show other false entries made by the same servant? (19.)

19. What are the presumptions as to post letters? (20, 21).

20. Explain the presumption, *Omnia rite esse acta*. (Broom's Maxims.)

21. What is meant by hearsay evidence? When is it admitted? (22-57, 162-164.)

22. What are admissions? Are they evidence for, or against, the party who makes them? How may they be made, and by whom? (23-28.)

23. Can a letter marked " Without prejudice " be used as evidence in a civil action? (*Walker* v. *Wilsher*, 58 L. J., Q. B., 501.)

24. When is a confession admitted in evidence at a criminal trial? (28-32.)

25. Explain what is meant by a dying declaration, and when it can be used as evidence. (33, 34.)

26. What was decided in Price v. Torrington? (1 Smith's Leading Cases.)

27. What rule is illustrated by Higham v. Ridgway? (36-39; 2 Smith's Leading Cases.)

28. When are statements by a deceased person, as to the contents of his will received in evidence? (40.)

29. Distinguish between a public and a general right. Under what conditions is hearsay evidence admitted in each case? (40-42.)

30. Under what circumstances is hearsay evidence admitted in questions of pedigree? (42-44.)

31. When can evidence given by a witness (who is now dead) at a previous trial be used? (44, 45.)

32. Can a bank be compelled to produce its books in an action between A and B? (49.)

33. Is a copy of entries in a banker's books evidence in legal proceedings? (49.)

34. Under what circumstances is a judgment a conclusive estoppel? (50-57.)

35. When may a witness depose to his " opinion " on a matter? (58-63.) What is the leading case on evidence of opinions? (75.)

36. When is evidence of character admissible (1) in criminal, (2) in civil trials? (64-66.)

37. Of what matters does the Court take judicial notice? (67.)

38. Need evidence be given of facts which are admitted (1) in civil, (2) in criminal trials? (70.)

39. What is meant by saying that oral evidence must be direct? (71.)

40. In what two ways may the contents of a document be proved? (72.)

41. What is meant by primary evidence? (72.)

42. When must you call the attesting witness to prove · the execution of a document? How do you prove it if the witness cannot be found? (73, 74.) Are there any exceptions to the rule? (75, 92.)

43. In what ways may you prove a document which does not require attestation to make it valid? (76.)

44. What do you understand by secondary evidence? (76.)

45. Enumerate the cases in which secondary evidence of a document can be given? (76-78.)

46. What steps would you take to enable you to give secondary evidence of a document which is in possession (1) of the other party; (2) of a stranger? (79.)

47. How do you prove the contents of (1) any public document; (2) a record; (3) a statute; (4) an order of the Privy Council or a Government department; (5) a foreign or colonial judgment? (81-90.)

48. Is there any presumption (1) as to the date of a document; (2) the order of execution of documents having the same date; (3) a stamp on a document; (4) sealing and delivery of a document professing to be a deed? (91, 92.)

49. When is a document said to prove itself? (92, 93.)

50. Is there any presumption as to the date of alterations in (1) a deed; (2) a will; (3) a simple contract? (94.)

51. When is parol evidence admitted with respect to a written document? (95-98.)

52. What evidence may be given to interpret the words used in a document? (99-101.)

53. If a lease of a rabbit warren contains a covenant to leave 10,000 rabbits, can oral evidence be given to show 1,000 rabbits means 1,200? (101.)

54. If the name of a legatee is left blank, can oral evidence be given to fill it in? (101.)

F

55. What is meant by the onus of proof? (105.)

56. On whom is the burden of proof? Show how the burden may be shifted from one side to the other? (106-108.)

57. Specify some of the chief presumptions. (111-115.)

58. What are the chief cases of estoppel *in pais?* (115-119.)

59. Enumerate the cases in which a person is incompetent to give evidence. (120-130.)

60. What communications are privileged from disclosure? (125, *et seq.*)

61. What questions may a witness refuse to answer? (131.)

62. In what cases is corroborative evidence needed? (132, 133.)

63. Is more than one witness ever necessary? (133, 134.)

64. When may evidence be given on affirmation instead of on oath? (135.)

65. In what ways may oral evidence be taken? (137.)

66. What matters can be dealt with in cross-examination and re-examination? (140.)

67. What is meant by a leading question? Can it be asked? (140.)

68. What is the object of cross-examination? (141.)

69. When may evidence be called to contradict answers to questions as to veracity of a witness? (142.)

70. What course can be adopted with an adverse witness by the party calling him? (193, 198.)

71. Can a witness refresh his memory by looking at a document? (146.)

72. What use can be made of depositions taken at a criminal enquiry before justices? (148.)

73. How do you perpetuate testimony in criminal cases? (149.)

74. What remedy is there for improper admission or rejection of evidence? (152.)

II.—QUESTIONS AND ANSWERS ON EVIDENCE.

Q. What is the difference between substantive and adjective law?

A. The former defines rights, duties, and liabilities. The latter comprises the mode of applying the former; and consists of (1) the rules of procedure which regulate litigation, (2) the rules of pleading, by which the material facts in issue are ascertained, and (3) the rules for proving those facts by evidence, presumptions, judicial notice, and inspection.

Q. What is meant by admissible evidence?

A. Any matter of fact of which the effect, tendency, or design is to produce in the mind a persuasion (affirmative or negative) of the existence of some other matter of fact (1 Benth. Jud. Ev., 17), which is in issue between the parties, or is relevant to the issue, and which is not excluded because of privilege, opinion, hearsay, character, or *res inter alios.*

Q. How do you determine the credit to be attached to human testimony?

A. (1) By correctly understanding the language used. (2) By judging the deportment of the witness, his previous veracity, and any interest or bias he possesses. (3) By judging the capacity of the witness as regards opportunity of observation, power of discernment, memory, and importance of the thing deposed to. (4) By weighing the consistency of the story, and its possibility or probability, or the contrary. (Best, 8th edition, pt. 1.)

Q. State and illustrate the rule as to best evidence.

A. The rule is that nothing but the highest quality of evidence which the nature of the case admits of will be allowed to be tendered. Thus the Judge and jury must not decide matters on their own knowledge (save points judicially noticed) ; the evidence must be original and not derivative (subject to the rule about secondary evidence of documents) :

and the evidence must be relevant. The rule is founded on the presumption that if inferior evidence is offered when evidence of a better nature can be obtained, the substitution of the former for the latter arises from fraud, or gross negligence, which is tantamount to fraud. To enable a person to give secondary evidence of a document he must show that he has done everything in his power to get the best or primary evidence, *e.g.*, if an original document is in his opponent's possession he must show that he has given a notice to produce before he can be entitled to give a copy in evidence. (Indermaur's Common Law, 448, 449; Best, bk. 1, pt. 1.)

Q. When is parol evidence admitted to explain, vary, or add to the terms of a written instrument ?

A. The general rule is that parol evidence is not admissible to vary, &c., the terms of a written contract (Burgess v. Wickham, 3 B. & S., 669). The exceptions are :—(*a*) In cases where terms are proved supplementary or collateral to so much of the agreement as is in writing ; (*b*) in cases where explanation of the terms of the contract is required ; (*c*) in the introduction of usages of trade or locality into the contract ; (*d*) in the application of equitable remedies in the case of mistake ; (*e*) to impeach the instrument for duress, fraud, or collusion. (Anson's Contracts, 261; Best, pt. 3, c. 1.)

Q. Apart from the pleadings, what means are available to each party for discovering, before the trial, the facts and documents on which the other side may rely ?

A. Discovery of facts, by interrogatories ; discovery of documents, by affidavit ; and inspection of documents, on notice or order. (Indermaur's Practice, 100-106.)

Q. Under what circumstances can an answer given by a witness in cross-examination be contradicted ?

A. It was enacted by the Common Law Procedure Act 1854, sec. 23, and the Criminal Evidence and Practice Amendment Act 1865, sec. 4, that " If a witness upon cross-examination as to a former statement made by him, relative to the subject matter of the cause, and inconsistent with his present testimony, does not distinctly admit that he has made such statement, proof may be given that he in fact did make it; but before such proof can be given, the circumstances of the supposed statement, sufficient to designate the particular occasion, must be mentioned to the witness, and he must be asked whether or not he has made such statement." But if the witness is asked a question merely intended to impeach his veracity, and not material to the subject matter of the case, evidence cannot be called to disprove such a statement, although it may be sometimes given to contradict an answer to a question which tends to impeach his general veracity. (Powell's Evidence, 526, 527.)

Q. What remedy is there for improper admission or rejection of evidence?

A. (1) In civil cases, an application may be made for a new trial if any substantial wrong or miscarriage of justice has taken place. (2) In criminal cases, after conviction, the Judge has power to state a case for the Court for Crown Cases Reserved, as this is a question of law arising at the trial (11 & 12 Vict., c. 78), irrespective of whether the prisoner was defended, or the objection was taken.

Q. Specify some of the statutory alterations in the law of evidence since 1837.

A. By 1 & 2 Vict., c. 105, persons are bound by oath administered in any form they consider binding. By 5 & 6 Vict., c. 69, persons entitled to property contingent on future events could file bills to perpetuate testimony. By 6 & 7 Vict., c. 85, criminals and interested persons not being parties, and by 14 & 15 Vict., c. 99, the parties to suits (except breach of promise and adultery cases) were made competent and compellable to give evidence, though not bound to answer any question tending to incriminate themselves. By 16 & 17 Vict., c. 83, husbands and wives of parties to civil suits were made competent and compellable witnesses, though not allowed to disclose communications made during marriage. By 17 & 18 Vict., c. 125, a witness in civil cases was allowed to affirm, extended to criminal cases by 24 & 25 Vict., c. 66; both replaced in 1869 by 32 & 33 Vict., c. 68, and now replaced by the Oaths Act 1888. By 17 & 18 Vict., c. 125 (civil), and 28 Vict., c. 18 (criminal), a party can discredit his "hostile" witness. By 32 & 33 Vict., c. 68, parties to actions for breach of promise to marry were made competent witnesses, but require corroboration, and parties to adultery cases and their husbands and wives are competent witnesses, but are not bound to confess adultery unless they have denied it in the witness box. By 42 Vict., c. 11, copies of entries in bankers' books are made evidence on certain conditions.

Q. What is a legal presumption? How many kinds of legal presumptions are there? Mention some of the more important presumptions.

A. An arbitrary inference expressly directed by the law to be drawn from certain facts. *Presumptiones juris et de jure*, which cannot be rebutted, and are therefore conclusive, *e.g.*, that a child under seven is incapable of committing a felony; and *presumptiones juris*, which are conclusive unless they are rebutted, *e.g.*, that a bill of exchange was given for value, that a person not heard of for seven years is dead, that an accused person is innocent, that persons who cohabit are married, that a child born in wedlock is legitimate. (Phipson, 2.)

Q. Distinguish between presumptions of law and presumptions of fact, and between conclusive and disputable presumptions of law.

A. Presumptions of fact are inferences of some fact from other facts that are known; they are rebuttable and, even if not rebutted, are not conclusive. Presumptions of law are (1) conclusive, *i.e.*, *presumptiones juris et de jure*, and these are irrebuttable, and arise when evidence is produced, the proof of which binds the Judge in law to regard some facts as proved beyond dispute ; (2) disputable, *i.e.*, *presumptiones juris*, which may be rebutted, but are conclusive until rebutted, *e.g.*, that a child born during wedlock is legitimate, that a child between seven and fourteen cannot commit crime; that a person is sane. (Stephen's Digest, cap. 1; Powell, 6th edition, 74.)

Q. What are the rules as to conflicting presumptions ?

A. (1) Special presumptions prevail over general ones, *e.g.*, a tidal stream is presumed to be navigable, but this may be rebutted by proving acts of ownership by riparian owners inconsistent with public rights. (2) Presumptions derived from the course of nature are stronger than casual presumptions. (3) Presumptions are favoured which give validity to acts. (4) The law presumes innocence. (Best, 311, 317.)

Q. Mention the chief presumptions relating to infancy.

A. If the infant is under seven years of age he cannot be convicted of crime, for the law considers him *doli incapax* and this presumption cannot be rebutted. Between seven and 14, although still *doli incapax*, the presumption may be rebutted by clear evidence that he knew that he was doing wrong, for *malitia supplet ætatem*, except in the case of rape. After 14, he is liable for all his crimes, except those of mere omission, as non-repair of a highway ; and after 21 all privilege of infancy ceases. Males under 14 and females under 12 cannot consent to marriage. (Thwaites' Criminal Guide, 12, 13.)

Q. Name some presumptions usually met with in practice.

A. (1) All persons in the realm are presumed to know the laws of the realm which have been duly promulgated. (2) Children under seven cannot commit crime. (3) Payment of money is presumptive evidence of a debt. (4) The law presumes innocence. (5) Ambiguous acts are presumed to be lawful. (6) Fraud and deceit and immorality are never presumed. (7) Marriage is presumed from cohabitation and reputation, except in bigamy cases and when damages for adultery are claimed. (8) Children born during wedlock are presumed to be legitimate. (9) *Omnia præsumuntur rite esse acta*—*e.g.*, documents 30 years old, coming from the proper custody, prove themselves. (10) Possession is *primâ facie* evidence of ownership. (11) A letter duly posted is presumed to have been delivered in the ordinary course. (12) A person not heard of for seven years is presumed to be dead. (13) *Omnia præsumuntur contra spoliatorem*, *e.g.*, Armory v. Delamirie, 1 Smith's L. C. (14) A person's residence is presumed to be his domicile. (15) A man is presumed to intend the reasonable consequences of his acts.

Q. What is meant by "the burthen of proof"? How is this burthen determined? Give examples.

A. It means the obligation resting on a litigant of proving affirmatively his case. A man who brings another before a judicial tribunal must rely on the strength of his own right and the clearness of his own proof, and not on the want of right or weakness of proof in his adversary. The burthen of proof usually lies on the plaintiff, but not always, thus if an indorsee of a bill of exchange sues the acceptor, and the defendant admits the drawing, accepting, and indorsing to the plaintiff, but alleges that it was obtained by fraud, of which the plaintiff had notice, here the burthen of proof is on the defendant. (Best, 260, 261; Indermaur's Common Law, 476, 477.)

Q. Explain how the burden of proof may be affected by presumptions of law.

A. The onus is on the party who but for evidence would fail. Thus a person suing for a debt must prove the contracting of the debt as well as non-payment. But the law presumes a bill of exchange was given for value until the contrary is shown; therefore, if the holder sues the acceptor, the burden will lie on the defendant to prove want of consideration, and then will be shifted back to the plaintiff to show he gave value for the bill. (Indermaur's Principles of Common Law, 477.)

Q. Action for goods sold and delivered. Defence : Statute of Limitations. On whom is the burden of proof ? Who has the right to begin ?

A. The burden of proof is on the defendant, and he, therefore, has the right to begin at the trial. (Indermaur's Practice, 139.)

Q. Which party has the right to begin at the trial?

A. In criminal cases, the prosecution. In civil cases, the plaintiff, if the onus of proving any one of the issues rests on him, or if he claims unliquidated and substantial damages ; in other cases, the defendant. In revocation of patents, the defendant, 46 & 47 Vict., c. 57, sec. 26. In probate suits, the party propounding the will, unless testamentary capacity and valid execution are admitted. (Best, 269, 587 ; Phipson, 17.)

Q. What are the rules as to the right of reply at a trial?

A. (1) If evidence is given to the jury (except as to character) by the party which did not begin, the other side has a right of reply. (2) In cases of joint defendants or prisoners, if some call evidence and others not, the party which began replies to the former, but the latter address the jury last. (3) If the party which did not begin calls no evidence, that party addresses the jury last, except (*a*) in Crown prosecutions, when the Attorney or Solicitor-General has the right to the last word, (*b*) if a prisoner makes a statement to the jury. (Phipson, 19, 20.)

Q. Of what matters is evidence unnecessary ?

A. (1) Matters admitted for the purpose of the trial. (2) Matters judicially noted.

Q. How are admissions made to save proof at the trial ?

A. In civil actions (except probate suits, divorce suits, and peerage claims), admissions may be made (1) by the pleadings, (2) by notice to admit facts under Order XXXII., (3) by agreement. In criminal proceedings, by a plea of guilty only.

Q. Of what matters must the Court take judicial notice ?

A. (1) The law and customs of England, the Supreme Court Rules, &c., but not Scotch, colonial, or foreign law. (2) Constitutional, political, and administrative matters, *e.g.*, accession of the Sovereign, existence of a recognised foreign State, officers of State. (3) Territorial and geographical divisions, *e.g.*, counties, parishes, but not of the situation or boundaries of a particular place. (4) The official gazettes. (5) Official seals and signatures. (6) Notorious facts, *e.g.*, the course of nature, coins, standards of weights and measures. (Phipson, cap. 2.)

Q. What are the chief functions of a Judge on a trial at nisi prius ?

A. He has to preside at the trial and to determine on the admissibility or inadmissibility of evidence tendered, also to check any irrelevant or improper examination or cross-examination. He should protect a witness from answering questions which may tend to criminate him. He explains any points occurring on which the jury require assistance. He sums up the case to the jury and directs them on the law and on the points as to which their verdict is required. After verdict he gives judgment, and, if necessary, considers and decides on the matter of costs. (Phipson, 3.)

Q. What generally are the respective functions of the Judge and the jury in trials at nisi prius? Illustrate your answer by showing their respective functions in cases where (1) *"probable cause,"* (2) *"reasonableness of belief or suspicion,"* and (3) *" contributory negligence" arise.*

A. The rule is that matters of law are determined by the

Judge, and matters of fact by the jury. Whether there is *any* evidence, is for the Judge; whether it is *sufficient*, for the jury. The Judge must explain (and the jury regard) any specific rule or presumption of law which may affect the evidence adduced. The Judge also determines certain facts, viz: (1) whether the facts as found by the jury do, or do not, amount to reasonable and probable cause in actions for malicious prosecution and false imprisonment; (2) what is a reasonable time for doing an act; (3) the existence of all facts on which depend the admissibility of evidence; (4) the construction of written documents, though not of peculiar or technical terms. Point (1) is for the jury to decide, except in the two actions named above; (2) is a question for the jury; (3) is a question for the jury, unless the Judge decides there is no evidence of it. (Phipson, 3.)

Q. What use can be made of depositions taken before a committing magistrate?

A. Under 11 & 12 Vict., c. 42, sec. 17, in indictable offences a deposition taken before justices can be used at the trial, on proof that the witness is dead, or too ill to travel, or kept out of the way, or insane, and that it purports to be signed by the justice before whom it was taken, and that it was taken in the presence of the party against whom it is used, and such party had full opportunity to cross-examine. A deposition for perpetuation of testimony in criminal cases under 30 & 31 Vict., c. 35, sec. 6, can be used at the trial if the deponent is dead or too ill to travel, and it purports to be signed by the justice taking it, and reasonable notice in writing was given to the other side, who had full opportunity to cross-examine. (Stephen's Digest, 148-150.)

Q. Can a witness be cross-examined as to previous statements in writing?

A. Yes, without such writing being shewn to him. But, if it is intended to contradict him by putting in the writing, his attention must first be called to those parts of the writing which are going to be used. Further, the Judge at any stage of the trial can inspect the writing and may then use it for the purpose of the trial at his discretion. 17 & 18 Vict., c. 125, sec. 24, as to civil cases, extended to criminal cases by 28 Vict., c. 18. These enactments overruled the answers given by the Judges to the House of Lords, in Queen Caroline's Case, 2 B. & B., 286.

Q. What do you understand by secondary evidence? Give the general rules applicable to its admissibility.

A. Any evidence which falls short of primary evidence, *i.e.*, of the best evidence. The rule is that it cannot be admitted until it is shewn that primary evidence is not obtainable. Secondary evidence of the contents of a document is admitted—(1) If the original is destroyed or lost; (2) if its production is physically impossible (characters traced on a rock) or highly inconvenient (words cut on a tombstone); (3) records and other public documents, which may usually be proved by office copies or examined copies; (4) a previous conviction or acquittal proved by a certificate, 14 & 15 Vict., c. 99, sec. 13; (5) entries in bankers' books under 42 Vict., c. 11; (6) if in possession of the adverse party, who declines to produce it; (7) if in possession of a third party who cannot be compelled to produce it, and appearing to a *subpœna duces tecum* claims the right to withhold it; (8) if there is a presumption of law that the document exists; (9) if the papers are voluminous and only their general result has to be proved; and (10) on examination of a witness on the *voir dire*—*i.e.*, a preliminary examination to judge of his competency to give testimony. As to oral testimony, secondary evidence is only admitted if the witness gave testimony on oath in a judicial proceeding in which the adverse litigant had power to cross-examine, and the witness cannot now be called, and the suit is substantially between the same parties and on the same matters. (Taylor, 396, 423.)

Q. How, and when, may secondary evidence be given of a document which has been lost or destroyed?

A. By any possible means, *e.g.*, a copy, draft, recollection of a person who knew its contents. It must be shown that the original did once exist, and that it has been destroyed or is lost, *i.e.*, that unsuccessful search has been made where it is most likely to be found. (Taylor, 397.)

Q. How, and when, may secondary evidence be given of a document which is in possession of the other side?

A. By any means the circumstances allow. Prove that the document is in the possession of the other side, and that you have served a notice to produce it. (Taylor, 406-418.)

Q. A document which A, a party to an action, wishes to give in evidence, is in the possession of B, who is not a party to the action. What proceedings should A take to have the document at the trial? Should B refuse to produce the document, has A any remedy?

A. He should issue a *subpœna duces tecum* and serve it on B. If B, being bound to produce the document, does not do so, A may sue B for damages and B is also liable to attachment. The Court may order a postponement of the trial to allow of the production of the document. Secondary evidence is not here admissible, unless the witness is under no legal obligation to produce the document. (Stephen's Digest, 77, 79 ; Powell, 399 ; Phipson, 379.)

Q. What documents may a witness refuse to produce?

A. A witness, if a stranger, cannot be compelled to produce the title deeds of his property, nor documents in the nature of title deeds. Nor can a party be compelled to produce documents which he swears relate solely to his own title or case, and do not tend to prove or support the case of his opponent; this privilege is not confined to title deeds only. Nor can production be compelled of a document which if produced would expose the witness to crimination, penalty, or forfeiture. Also where a principal would be entitled to refuse production of a document, it cannot be compelled from his solicitor, trustee or mortgagee. (Phipson, 110; Best, pt. 3, c. 1.)

Q. Explain the term " hearsay evidence," showing when such evidence is admissible.

A. Hearsay evidence is some oral or written statement of a person, who is not produced in Court, conveyed to the Court either by a witness or by the instrumentality of a document. The rule is to reject it as being " second hand ' evidence not connected by responsible testimony with the party against whom it is offered. It is admissible (1) in matters of public or general interest ; (2) in cases of pedigree ; (3) where it forms part of the *res gestæ*; (4) where it consists of an entry or statement made by a person in the course of business and discharge of duty (Price v. Lord Torrington), or contrary to his pecuniary or proprietary interest (Higham v. Ridgway) ; (5) evidence of a dead witness on a former trial between the same parties; (6) ancient documents to prove ancient possession; (7) books of a dead incumbent containing payments and receipts relating to the benefice ; and (8) dying declarations in trials for homicide. (Best, 439-458 ; Indermaur's Principles of Common Law, 451-457.)

Q. State (1) on what grounds, (2) with what limitations, (3) in what forms, hearsay evidence is admissible in matters of public and general interest.

A. (1) That the origin of the rights claimed is usually of so ancient a date, and the rights are of so undefined and general a character that direct proof of their existence and nature can seldom be obtained and ought not to be required; that all persons must be deemed conversant with matters in which the community are interested ; that common rights are naturally discussed in public, and their nature lessens the chance of personal bias, and therefore what is uttered in conversation about them may be presumed true ; that the general interest of the subject would call forth immediate contradiction to a false statement; that reputation can hardly exist without the concurrence of many unconnected though interested persons; that such concurrence is strong presumptive evidence of truth, and that the prevailing current of assertion is used as evidence. (2) The limitations are (*a*) to public or general interest as distinct from private rights; (*b*) in public interest, *e.g.*, claim of highway, the evidence of anybody is admitted, but in general interest, *e.g.*, boundary of a parish, the evidence must be from persons having local knowledge, the declaration must have been made before any controversy arose, it is admissible if made with the view of preventing a dispute and although in direct support of the declarant's title, and is not to be rejected if the declarant stood *in pari jure* with the party tendering the evidence. (3) Both oral and documentary declarations, *e.g.*, deeds, leases, copies thereof, maps if prepared by persons acquainted with the district, a verdict or judgment on the matter in issue. (Taylor, 537-559.)

Q. State (1) *on what grounds,* (2) *with what limitations,* (3) *in what forms, hearsay evidence is admissible in declarations against interest.*

A. (1) The extreme improbability of its falsehood. (2) The declarant must be shown to be dead, he need not have had positive personal knowledge, the entry must be against his interest, that interest must be pecuniary or proprietary, the entry must completely charge the declarant, the whole entry is admitted (Higham v. Ridgway). (3) Whether oral or written, R. v. Buckley, 13 Cox, 293. (Taylor, 588, *et seq.*; 2 Smith's Leading Cases.)

Q. State (1) *on what grounds,* (2) *with what limitations,* (3) *in what forms hearsay evidence is admissible in matters of pedigree.*

A. (1) Necessity—for, as facts must often be proved which occurred many years before the trial and were known to few, strict adherence to ordinary rules of evidence might often occasion failure of justice. (2) The limitations are to hearsay proceeding from persons who were *de jure* related to the family in question, as they would have the greatest interest in seeking, the best opportunity for obtaining, and the least reason for falsifying, information on the subject. The declarant must be proved to be such a relation by evidence independent of the declaration; the declaration must have been made *ante litem motam*, but is not rejected if made to prevent litigation, or if living testimony could be called; the declarations may relate to the general facts of descent and relationship or to the particular facts and times and places of birth, marriage or death, but must be confined to facts immediately connected with the pedigrees; and the proof of the declaration must be required for a genealogical purpose. (3) Oral declarations of deceased relations; family conduct; entries in any book or paper by parents or relations; correspondence of deceased relations; recitals in settlements, family deeds and wills, inscriptions on tombstones, &c. (Taylor, 560, 579.)

Q. State (1) *on what grounds,* (2) *with what limitations,* (3) *in what forms, hearsay evidence is admissible in declarations in the course of office or business.*

A. The rule as laid down in Price v. Lord Torrington (1 S.L.C., 352) and other cases is that such entries will be admitted when made strictly in the course of business or discharge of duty. Nothing beyond this will be admitted. The entry must have been made at the time of the event occurring, and must have been made in the due discharge of the business about which the person is employed, and the duty must be to do the very thing to which the entry relates and then to make a record of it. The grounds of admission are that there may be no other evidence, and the probability of the account being true or false is neither greater nor less than the probability of the person being honest or dishonest which is nothing more than may be said of every case of hearsay. (See Notes in 1 Smith's L. C., 353 *et seq.*)

Q. What is meant by secondary evidence of oral testimony? When and how can this kind of evidence be made available?

A. Any evidence falling short of the oral evidence of the person who actually gave such testimony. If a witness has given his evidence on oath in a judicial proceeding in which the adverse litigant had power to cross-examine, the testimony so given will, if the witness himself cannot be called, be admitted in any subsequent suit between the same parties or the persons claiming under them, provided it relates to the same subject or substantially involves the same material points. (Taylor, 249.)

Q. When, and with what limitations, are "dying declarations" receivable in evidence?

A. They are admissible in trials for homicide only, where the death of the declarant is the subject of enquiry and the circumstances of the death are the subject of the declaration. It must be proved that the declarant had a settled expectation, that he would not recover, and has since died. The grounds for admission appear to be (1) *Nemo moriturus presumitur mentiri;* (2) the difficulty of getting better proof; (3) the witness' lack of interest in perverting the words used. (Best, 443 ; Stephen's Digest, 33.)

Q. Explain Res inter alios acta alteri nocere non debet.

A. No person is to be affected by the words or acts of others, unless he is connected with them either personally, or by those whom he represents, or by whom he is represented. If A sues B for goods sold, and B's defence is that the sale was on certain terms, B cannot give evidence that A has sold similar goods to strangers on those terms. Exceptions to the rule are (1) to prove existence of malice, knowledge, intent, motive, or any bodily or mental state; (2) to prove guilty knowledge of a receiver of stolen goods; (3) to prove an organised plan or scheme of operation, *e.g.*, fraud or to negative accident. (Best, 452-62; Stephen, 14-21.)

Q. Is the opinion of a witness evidence?

A. Not as a rule, for the witness must depose to facts. Exceptions exist: (1) as to the identification of a person, thing, or handwriting; (2) as to the apparent condition of a person (drunk or sober), or thing (good or bad repair of a house); (3) opinions of experts on matters of science, skill, trade, and foreign law; (4) character. (Best, 465-472; Powell, 111-118; Stephen, 57-62; Phipson, 254-273.)

Q. Define admissions. By whom may they be made, and what is their effect when given in evidence?

A. The term "admissions" means the mutual concessions which the parties to an action make in the course of their pleadings, the effect of which is to narrow the area of facts or allegations requiring to be proved by evidence. Counsel may at a trial bind their clients by any admissions which they in their discretion see fit to make. An agent can only bind his principal by admission when it comes within the scope of his authority, and a wife can only bind her husband when she has authority (express or implied) so to do. An infant cannot make admissions, nor can his guardian or next friend generally do so for him. The effect of admissions is to bind the party making them, unless he can show surprise or mistake, or other sufficient reason. (Indermaur's Common Law, 480-482.)

Q. What is an estoppel? How many kinds are there?

A. An admission (or something which the law treats as an admission) of so conclusive a kind that the party affected by it is not permitted to contradict it, although he may show that the party setting it up is himself estopped from taking advantage of it. (2 Smith's Leading Cases, 693.) It is based on the maxim *Allegans contraria non est audiendus.* Estoppels must be reciprocal if both parties are intended to be bound; usually affect only the parties and their privies and not strangers; and conflicting estoppels neutralize each other. Three—by matter of record, *e.g.*, a judgment; by deed; and *in pais*, *i.e.*, by conduct. A record is not an estoppel if obtained by fraud or collusion (Duchess of Kingston's Case, 2 Smith's L. C., 812); a deed is not an estoppel if obtained by fraud or duress or tainted with illegality. (Collins v. Blantern, 1 Smith's L. C., 398.)

Q. What are the rules which regulate the admission of confessions in criminal cases?

A. The confession must have been purely voluntary. So that if the confession was made because of any inducement of a temporal nature having reference to the charge and held out by a person in authority (*e.g.*, prosecutor or constable) it is not admissible; but any facts discovered by the aid of such inadmissible confession can be used. (Rex v. Warwickshell, Leech, 263.)

Q. On what principle and with what limitations are admissions and confessions received?

A. The ground of reception is that a party's declaration may be presumed to be true as against himself; but no presumption of truth arises with regard to declarations made by the party or his agents in his favour. In order to be received they must have been made voluntarily, and not in consequence of any threat, promise, or the like; for in the latter case, the party making them may have been induced, by hope or fear, to criminate himself falsely. They only affect the party and not third persons. (Phipson, 122, 154.)

Q. What kinds of evidence are excluded on grounds of public policy?

A. (1) Evidence which would be prejudicial to the public service; (2) evidence which discloses the means by which information for the detection of crime was obtained; (3) evidence which discloses what the witness did in a judicial capacity; (4) statements by a parent to bastardize his off-spring; (5) communications to legal advisers, but not to medical or spiritual advisers; and (6) communications between husband and wife. (Best, 529-536; Phipson, 93.)

Q. What matters are not provable by a single witness?

A. (1) In trials for treason or misprision of treason one witness is not sufficient. (2) In trials for perjury one witness is not sufficient unless there are circumstances proved which corroborate such witness. (3) In breach of promise cases the evidence of the plaintiff must be corroborated by some other material evidence. (4) In bastardy proceedings the evidence of the mother must be corroborated in some material particular. (5) Orders for the removal of paupers, 39 & 40 Vict., c. 61, sec. 34. (6) Offences under the Criminal Law Amendment Act 1885, sec. 4, and the Cruelty to Children Act 1889, if the proof rests on unsworn testimony of children. (7) As regards the evidence of an accomplice, it is the duty of the Judge to warn the jury that it is unsafe to convict without corroboration though they have a legal right to do so. (8) It is a rule of practice to require corroboration in cases of claims to the property of dead persons. (9) Wills. (Stephen's Digest, 132-134; Phipson, 357, 358; Best, 551-569.)

Q. What persons are now excluded from being witnesses in civil cases?

A. Formerly parties to actions, and their husbands and wives, and any persons interested, and criminals and atheists, could not give evidence, but they may do so now (6 & 7 Vict., c. 85; 14 & 15 Vict., c. 99; 16 & 17 Vict., c. 83; 32 & 33 Vict., c. 68; 51 & 52 Vict., c. 46). But in proceedings instituted in consequence of adultery a party to the suit cannot be asked a question tending to show that he or she has committed adultery, unless such witness has already given evidence in disproof of adultery (32 & 33 Vict., c. 68).

Husbands and wives are not compellable to disclose communications made by one to the other during marriage (16 & 17 Vict., c. 83). An idiot is incapable of giving evidence; and so also is a lunatic, except during a lucid interval. A person deaf, dumb, and blind cannot give evidence. A young child incapable of understanding the nature of an oath cannot give evidence. (Indermaur's Principles of Common Law, 452-462.)

Q. What persons are incompetent to give evidence in criminal trials?

A. The accused and his wife (or husband) cannot give evidence—except in high treason; in proceedings for personal injuries done by one to the other; in indictments for non-repair of a highway or bridge, or for nuisance to a highway, river, or bridge, or for trying civil rights only (40 & 41 Vict., c. 14); on a charge of sending an unseaworthy ship to sea (38 & 39 Vict., c. 88, sec. 4); under the Sale of Food and Drugs Act 1875; under the Conspiracy and Protection of Property Act 1875; under the Army Discipline Act 1879 on a charge of unlawful possession of arms, &c.; under the Explosive Substances Act 1883 (46 Vict., c. 3, sec. 4); under the Married Women's Property Act 1884 in criminal proceedings by a husband against his wife, (or *vice versâ*) in respect of a crime done by one to the other's property while they are living apart, or at the moment of desertion; under the Criminal Law Amendment Act 1885 on a charge of rape, or indecent assault upon a female, or abduction, or any offence under that Act; under the Merchandise Marks Act 1887; in libel (Libel Act 1888); and under the Cruelty to Children Act 1889. A child of tender years cannot give evidence if it does not understand the duty of speaking the truth; nor can a felon sentenced to death; nor idiots and lunatics, for they lack understanding. Solicitor and counsel of the accused cannot give evidence as to knowledge acquired in that capacity,

unless their client waives his privilege, or consulted them to
obtain information which would enable him to commit the
crime. (Reg. v. Cox, 54 L. J., M. C., 41.)

*Q. Describe the questions which a witness may decline to
answer on the ground of privilege.*

A. There are two chief cases of privilege, viz. :—(1) On
the ground that answering the question may tend to criminate
him or expose him to a penalty, which is a matter to be con-
sidered and determined by the Judge (*Ex parte* Reynolds ;
51 L. J., Ch., 766). (2) On the ground of the matter
embracing a professional communication between counsel,
solicitors or their clerks, and a client. The privilege here is
the client's, who may waive it, and for this ground of
privilege to exist professional employment and confidence
are essential (Reg. v. Cox & Railton, 15 Cox's Criminal
Cases, 611). A further ground of privilege of an exceptional
nature is that of matters relating to affairs of State.
(Indermaur's Principles of Common Law, 471-476.)

Q. What questions may a witness refuse to answer ?

A. (1) Questions the answers to which may in the
opinion of the Judge tend to criminate him or subject him
to a penalty, or to a forfeiture, but not questions which
expose him to a civil suit (46 Geo. III., c. 37). (2) Questions
upon confidential conversations between legal adviser and
client (see hereon Reg. v. Cox, 14 Q.B.D., 153.) (Stephen's
Digest of Evidence, 127-131.)

*Q. What is the practice as to the reception of statements
made by a prisoner when defended by counsel at a criminal
trial: (1) When no witnesses are called for the defence? (2)
When witnesses are called for the defence ?*

A. The rule as now laid down is, that in case (1) he may
make a statement to the jury at the conclusion of his counsel's
speech ; but in case (2) he cannot make any statement in
addition to his counsel's address. (Broom's Commentaries,
1055.)

Q. What communications, oral and written, are privileged from discovery?

A. (1) A witness is not compelled to answer any question or produce any document tending to incriminate him; (2) Counsel, solicitors, and their clerks are not permitted to disclose communications which have been made to them in professional confidence by their clients, without the consent of such clients, nor can the client himself be compelled to disclose such communications; any document prepared for obtaining the advice of a solicitor is privileged, whether laid before him or not; evidence obtained after litigation is threatened or begun; (3) Communications, the disclosure of which may be prejudicial to public interests. (Powell, cap. 7.)

Q. How do the rules of evidence differ in civil and criminal cases?

A. Civil issues may be proved by preponderance of evidence; criminal issues must be proved beyond reasonable doubt. The rules as to dying declarations, character, confessions, and incompetency of parties to give evidence are peculiar to criminal cases. At a criminal trial (1) more than one witness is sometimes required, *e.g.*, treason and perjury; (2) evidence of accomplices is viewed with suspicion; (3) confessions are received with great caution, must be purely voluntary, and are only admissible against the person making them; (4) a prisoner on his trial cannot give evidence, subject to the alteration made by the Criminal Law Amendment Act 1885, and some other statutes; (5) as a rule husband and wife may not give evidence against each other; (6) there is a difference as to the use of depositions; (7) dying declarations as to cause of death are admitted in cases of homicide; and (8) witnesses as to character are allowed.

Q. State the rules for examination-in-chief, cross-examination, and re-examination.

A. In examination-in-chief, all material facts to prove the party's case should be elicited by plain and direct questions, which must not be leading in their character, unless the witness is a hostile one. In cross-examination, all material facts for the cross-examiner's case not brought out by the examination-in-chief should be elicited, and questions may be asked to test the witness' veracity, and leading questions are here allowed. In re-examination, strictly only questions may be put on matters arising out of the cross-examination, and here again leading questions must not be put. Generally, the rules as to the non-admissibility of secondary and hearsay evidence must be observed. (Stephen's Digest, 139, *et seq.*)

Q. What is meant by leading questions? When may they be put?

A. Questions which suggest the answers desired from the witness. They may be asked in cross-examination, but not on examination-in-chief, except (1) to identify persons or things previously described; (2) if a witness is called to contradict another who has sworn to a certain fact, he may be asked if the fact ever occurred; (3) if a witness is hostile; (4) if the evidence is of a very complicated character, or the witness manifestly has a defective memory; (5) on introducing points to save time; and (6) on points which are not disputed.

Q. May a witness read his evidence?

A. No. But he can " refresh his memory " by looking at a writing made or examined by himself soon after the event which it records took place.

Q. How is the attendance of a witness procured?

A. In civil actions, by a writ of subpœna, which may be either *ad testificandum* (to give evidence) or *duces tecum* (to produce documents); the writ must be served personally; a reasonable sum for expenses must be tendered with it; disobedience exposes to (1) action for £10 penalty and further recompense under 5 Eliz., c. 9, s. 12, (2) action for damages, or (3) attachment for contempt of Court. Before justices of the peace, by summons or warrant. At criminal trials, a

witness who was called before justices attends on his recog-
nizance, or is committed to prison for safe custody ; other
witnesses are served with a Crown Office subpœna.

*Q. Is evidence admissible at a criminal trial which tends
to show that prisoner has committed other offences than the one
he is being tried for ?*

A. The prosecution cannot give such evidence for the
purpose of leading the jury to form the conclusion that the
prisoner is a person likely from his criminal conduct or
character to have committed the offence for which he is being
tried. But the bare fact of evidence tendered showing the
commission of other crimes does not make it inadmissible if it
is relevant to an issue before the jury ; and it is so relevant
if it bears on the question whether the act charged was
designed or accidental, or if it rebuts a defence which would
be open to the prisoner. (Makins v. Attorney General, *Law
Students' Journal*, February, 1894, p. 34.)

INDEX.

A

Abandoning part of claim or defence, 44
Abatement of nuisance, 58
Action—
    Sketch of, 6-11
    Preliminaries to, 22
    Joining different causes, 23
    Commencement of, appearance, judgment in default and under
        Order XIV., 25-32
    Pleadings, 32-38
    Interlocutory proceedings, 38-44
    Trial and subsequent proceedings, 44-54
    Miscellaneous points, 54-61
    Procedure from writ to judgment, 26
Adjective law, 67
Admissible evidence, 67
Admissions, how made, 74, 82
Advice on reading evidence, 3
Advice on reading procedure, 2
Agreement ousting jurisdiction of Court, 58, 59
Amendment of pleadings, 35
Appeal—
    From Master, 43
    From Judge, 43
    On question of costs, 52
    From Divisional Court, 53
    To Court of Appeal, 53
    From County Court, 61
Appearance, steps on default of entering, 28
Arbitration Act 1889, 43, 58, 59
Arresting defendant before judgment, 42
Attachment of debts, how obtained, 51
Attachment, writ of, 54

B

Bankruptcy, effect of, on action, 28
Best evidence—rule as to, 67
Burthen of proof, 72, 73

Q

R

S

T

Tender, 36

Third Party Procedure, 30

Tort—

    Remitting action to County Court, 41

Trial—

    Right to begin, 73
    Right to reply, 73
    Without pleadings, 37, 38
    Modes of, 44
    By jury in High Court, 45
       ,,   ,, County Court, 45
       ,, —sketch of proceedings at, 46

W

Withdrawal of a juror, 49

Witness—

    When more than one required, 84
    Questions he may refuse to answer, 86, 86
    May refresh his memory, 88

Witnesses—

    Mode of examination, 48
    Examination of, 48
    Cross-examination of, 48
    Treatment of adverse, 48
    How attendance procured, 48, 88
    When answers in cross-examination can be contradicted, 68
    Can be cross-examined as to previous written statements, 75
    Incompetency in civil cases, 84
       ,,   ,, criminal cases, 85

Writ of summons, 25

    To judgment, steps from, 26
    Renewal of, 29
    Concurrent, 29

GEO. BARBER, PRINTER, CURSITOR STREET, CHANCERY LANE.